Native Writers
VOICES OF POWER

Kim Sigafus

Lyle Ernst

NATIVE VOICES
Summertown, Tennessee

Library of Congress Cataloging-in-Publication Data

Sigafus, Kim.
    Native writers voices of power / Kim Sigafus, Lyle Ernst.
        p. cm. — (Native trailblazers)
    ISBN 978-0-9779183-8-6 (pbk.) — ISBN 978-1-57067-942-1 (e-book)
    1. American literature—Indian authors—Biography—Juvenile literature.   2. Indians
in literature.   I. Ernst, Lyle.   II. Title.
    PS153.I52S56 2012
    810.9'897—dc23
    [B]
                                                                    2011051617

© 2012 Kim Sigafus, Lyle Ernst
Cover and interior design: John Wincek

7th Generation,
a division of Book Publishing Company
PO Box 99
Summertown, TN 38483
888-260-8458
bookpubco.com

Printed in the United States.

ISBN: 978-0-9779183-8-6

16 15 14 13 12   1 2 3 4 5 6

Photo credits found on page 91.

Book Publishing Co. is a member of
Green Press Initiative. We chose to print
this title on paper with postconsumer
recycled content, processed without chlorine,
which saved the following natural resources:

32 trees

938 pounds of solid waste

14,809 gallons of water

3,284 pounds of greenhouse gases

13 million BTU of total energy

For more information, visit
greenpressinitiative.org.

Savings calculations thanks to the
Environmental Defense Paper Calculator,
edf.org/papercalculator.

To our spouses, Pat Ernst and Mike Sigafus. Their love, support, and understanding are what give us the ability to do what we love.

he writing of this book has been a journey for us, and we've gotten to know some very special people along the way. The voices of these authors will be heard long after they are no longer with us. They carry the voices of their people from both past and present and help preserve Native oral traditions.

We would especially like to thank our wonderful editor, Kathie Hanson, along with authors Joe Bruchac, Nicola Campbell, Marilyn Dumont, and Tim Tingle. They have been extremely helpful in making this book what it is.

We hope this book will become an inspiration to those who have yet to tell their stories. We are waiting and listening.

CONTENTS

Native Writers

VOICES OF POWER

INTRODUCTION

here have been entirely too many falsehoods and myths written about the Native people of the United States and Canada. The depiction of Native people depends entirely on the writer's perspective. For example, a 1704 French and Indian raid on colonial settlers in the village of Deerfield, Massachusetts, was described as a massacre, whereas the annihilation of a village of sleeping Cheyenne Indians in 1864 was celebrated as a victory over "hostiles." Both are examples of the European American historical perspective, which has also been prevalent in movies, making Hollywood one of the biggest sources of distorted facts and stereotypes about Indians.

A good way to look beyond these inaccurate depictions is to read the works of Native authors. Many of them share stories that have been passed down from generation to generation and told to them by their elders. In this book, you will read the life stories of ten Native writers and learn about their accomplishments. Although many of them write fiction and poetry, the stories they share provide a balanced and authentic expression of the experience of being a Native person. Some of the writers were interviewed for this book, while information about others is based on research. All of the biographies are accurate to the best of our knowledge.

While researching this book, we came to see that many Indian writers feel they have a responsibility to pass on the legacy and customs of their people. They also feel the need to contribute to a Native perspective and help set the record straight about the background and beliefs of Native people. In this way, they are teaching everyone who reads their stories.

We found the authors in this book truly inspirational. We hope you find them as interesting as we did.

Anthology. An anthology is a collection of various authors' selected writings, usually in the same literary form, written in the same time period, or on the same subject. An anthology can also be a collection of selected writings by one author.

Autobiography. An autobiography is similar to a biography except that an autobiography is written by the subject himself.

Bachelor's degree. A bachelor's degree is an academic degree from a college or university. The course work required for a bachelor's degree usually takes four years to complete.

Biography. A biography is a detailed description of someone's life. A biography tells the subject's life story by highlighting various parts of his or her life. Biographical works are usually nonfiction, but fiction can also be used to portray a person's life.

Creative writing. Creative writing is drama, fiction, or poetry that an author invents using his or her imagination (in addition to or in place of research). Creative writing is offered as a course of study.

Dissertation or thesis. A dissertation or thesis is a document written by a student seeking an academic degree. The document explains the student's research and findings on a particular subject. A written thesis is associated with a bachelor's or master's degree, and a written dissertation is normally associated with a doctorate degree.

Doctorate degree. A doctorate degree is the highest academic degree in any field of study. This degree is sometimes referred to as a PhD.

Fellowship. Fellowships are programs designed to provide financial grants that enable a person to set aside time for writing, research, travel, and general career advancement. An example is the National Endowment for the Arts Literature Fellowships program, which offers $25,000 grants to individuals.

Fiction. Fiction is an invented, imagined, or made-up story.

Folktale. A folktale is a traditional story that is usually narrated by a person who is not in the tale. Folktales can be written down, but they have often been handed down orally. Folktales include fables, fairy tales, legends, and myths.

Fulbright professor. A Fulbright professor is a professor who has received a prestigious award by the Fulbright Program. The purpose of the Fulbright Program is to increase mutual understanding between the people of the United States and people in other countries through travel and the exchange of knowledge and skills.

Graduate teaching assistant. A graduate teaching assistant is a graduate student who is employed for a temporary teaching position by a college or university. Graduate teaching assistants are not the main course instructors, but they assist the course professors. Teaching assistants sometimes receive a salary based on semester work.

Graduate teaching fellow. A graduate teaching fellow is a graduate student who is the primary instructor for a college course. Graduate teaching fellows do not assist other professors. Graduate fellows receive a salary (called "a fellowship") based on semester or yearly work.

Literature. Literature is the written word. It includes, but is not limited to, poetry, novels, histories, biographies, and essays.

Master's degree. A master's degree is an advanced university degree beyond a bachelor's degree. It is usually granted after two years of study in a specific field. A master's degree can mean an increase in salary or advanced job placement.

There are two types of master's degrees: a master of arts (MA) and a master of science (MS).

Mentor. A mentor is a trusted friend, counselor, or teacher who is usually a more experienced person. Some professions have mentoring programs in which newcomers are paired with more experienced people who advise them and serve as examples. Schools sometimes offer mentoring programs to new students or students having difficulties.

Narrative. A story that can be either true or fictitious.

Narrative poetry. Narrative poetry is a poem that tells a story. Narrative poems can be short, long, simple, or complicated, such as epics and ballads. Some narrative poems take the form of a novel that rhymes. Shorter narrative poems can be similar to a short story.

Narrator. A narrator is the person telling a story. Narration can take different forms: A first-person narrator is the person telling a story and also a character in the story being told. A second-person narrator is a character in a story that refers to the reader as "you." This reference makes the reader feel as if he or she is a character in the story being told. A third-person narrator is a person telling the story but is not a character in the story being told.

Nonfiction. Nonfiction works are based on facts and reality. They include biographies, histories, and opinions. Nonfiction works are written in prose.

Novel. A novel is a story of considerable length that is not true but rather created by the author. A novel has characters and tells a story that follows a series of action and scenes.

Pell Grant. A Pell Grant is a sum of money given to a student who needs help paying for college. To be eligible, students must show financial need and be enrolled in a college where they are earning their first bachelor's degree. The grant is sponsored by the United States Department of Education, which determines student need with a standard formula using information that students supply on the Free Application for Federal Student Aid (FAFSA).

Poetry. Poetry is the use of language for an imaginative experience expressed through meaning, sound, and rhythm. Poetic word choices evoke an emotional response. Poetry can rhyme but it is not necessary. Formal poetry often has meter or a specifically structured rhythmic pattern.

Prose. Prose is the ordinary form of spoken or written language. Unlike formal poetry, prose does not follow any particular structure, rhythm, or rhyme scheme.

Pulitzer Prize. The Pulitzer Prize is an award for achievements in newspaper and online journalism, literature, and musical composition in the United States. Prizes are awarded yearly in twenty-one categories. In twenty of the categories, each winner receives a certificate and a $10,000 cash award. The winner in the public service category of the journalism competition is awarded a gold medal.

Screenplay. A screenplay or script is a written work that is created for a film or television program. Screenplays can be original works or adaptations from existing pieces of writing.

Sensory words. Sensory words are usually adjectives that refer to the five senses: taste, touch, sight, smell, and sound.

Tone. Tone is the attitude a writer takes toward a subject or character. Tone can be serious, solemn, objective, humorous, sarcastic, ironic, satirical, or tongue-in-cheek.

University fellowship. A university fellowship is a monetary award used to recruit outstanding students to advanced degree programs. A fellowship usually includes a living expense allowance, paid tuition, and other university expenses.

Verse. A verse is a line of poetry.

Writer in residence. A writer in residence is an accomplished writer who is invited to live and teach at a college or university for a certain period of time. Students benefit from the insights that writers in residence share with them.

Sherman Alexie

T o call Sherman Alexie a man of many words would be an understatement. He began writing poetry while in college and then expanded into writing short stories, novels, and screenplays. With time, he evolved into an editor, musician, lecturer, movie producer, director, and, eventually, stand-up comedian.

Born October 7, 1966, on the Spokane Indian Reservation in Wellpinit, Washington, Sherman Joseph Alexie Jr. is a Spokane and Coeur d'Alene Indian. He prefers the term "Indian" to "Native American." Sherman was once quoted as saying "Indians call each other Indians. Native American is a guilty white liberal thing." Sherman was raised on the reservation. His father held numerous jobs, including truck driver and logger. His mother was a social worker.

Sherman Alexie

Sherman was born with hydrocephalus, a serious physical condition sometimes referred to as "water on the brain." The fluid surrounding the brain normally travels through the brain and then drains away to be absorbed in the bloodstream. If there is a blockage or if too much fluid is produced and cannot be absorbed, then hydrocephalus occurs. The buildup of liquid puts pressure on the brain and can push it against the skull.

When Sherman was six months old, his doctors recommended that Sherman have brain surgery to relieve the pressure caused by the built-up fluid in his skull. They told his parents that they didn't expect Sherman to survive the surgery, and that if he did, he would probably be severely handicapped. Sherman must have had a strong will to live. Not only did he pull through the surgery, but he also wasn't handicapped. Although he didn't lose any physical or mental capabilities, he did suffer from violent seizures throughout much of his childhood.

Despite his physical ailments, Sherman was a quick learner. He began to read at age three, and when he was five he read a 619-page edition of John Steinbeck's classic novel *The Grapes of Wrath*. Because he was such a good reader at an early age, and because of his seizures, he was considered an outcast and was picked on a lot by other children. His experiences of growing up poor and feeling like an outsider on the Spokane Indian Reservation are included in his award-winning young-adult novel, *The Absolutely True Diary of a Part-Time Indian*.

Sherman's grandmother had a huge influence on his early life. He called her "Big Mom" and she called him "Junior." She told him humorous stories about his tribe and loved to bring books for him to read. Often these were books she found while shopping at garage sales or the Goodwill store. Unfortunately, they weren't always books that Sherman wanted to read. Big Mom didn't bother to see what the books were about. She brought home everything from Harlequin romances to auto-repair books. It was important to her for Junior to have enough to read.

Sherman attended the reservation grade school and planned to attend the reservation high school. Shortly after enrolling there, however, he found his mother's name in one of his textbooks. When he realized the same textbook had been used at the school for over thirty years, he decided he'd receive a better education if he went to high school off the reservation. He transferred to Reardan High School in Reardan, Washington, where he was the only Indian student.

All the students at Reardan High were white, and the town, which was surrounded by farms, had only white residents. Life on the reservation had been isolating for Sherman, and he was afraid of anything new and different, especially white girls. He was terrified of them. But in time he found it natural to hang out with students who were bookworms, members of the drama club, basketball players, and even future farmers. He was exposed to many more types of people and ways of life than he'd experienced while growing up on the reservation.

Sherman studied hard and was selected captain of the school's basketball team. He still enjoys pointing out that the mascot for the team was an Indian. He remains a huge basketball fan and to this day plays with some buddies in Seattle. "Basketball is born of poverty," he says. "A hoop can be made from anything." He knows this from experience: his first basketball was made from a roll of duct tape, and his hoop was a coffee can with both ends cut out and nailed to a tree.

His hard work and perseverance in high school paid off, and Sherman graduated as class valedictorian in 1985. He received a scholarship to Gonzaga University in Spokane, Washington. Two years later he decided he wanted to be a doctor, so he transferred to Washington State University in Pullman, Washington, to pursue medicine. That didn't last long. After fainting several times in anatomy class, he realized he needed to find a different career. He wasn't certain what he wanted to study until one day he stumbled upon a creative writing and poetry class. He already loved poetry and had an aptitude for writing, so he enrolled. Eventually he graduated from college with a bachelor's degree in American studies.

Sherman's decision to change his course of study was a good one. After graduating from Washington State University, he was awarded poetry fellowships from the Washington

State Arts Commission and the National Endowment for the Arts.

Writing is not an easy task, even for a successful author like Sherman. He works hard at his trade, and because of this he sometimes considers writing a burden. Despite his success, Sherman still feels anxious when his books are reviewed. He was very nervous when the *New York Times Book Review* was going to evaluate *The Business of Fancy-dancing*, one of his early books of poems and short stories. He worked himself into such a state of fearful expectation that even though the book received a positive review, Sherman went into the bathroom and was sick after reading the reviewer's comments.

One of Sherman's passions is writing for young people, but he has been accused of overemphasizing the harsh realities that kids sometimes face. In the June 9, 2011, edition of the *Wall Street Journal*, Sherman defended his perspective in an essay titled "Why the Best Kids' Books Are Written in Blood." In the essay he wrote about being the speaker at an alternative high school graduation ceremony. All the students in the class came from backgrounds that included abuse, suicide, racism, and absentee parents, and they had all read *The Absolutely True Diary of a Part-Time Indian*. Sherman explained that the kids listening to his speech appreciated his honest portrayal of the teen in his book, whose experiences mirrored many of their own.

Reviewers have accused Sherman of "depravity" and "hideously distorted portrayals" in his young-adult literature. His response to those critics is to point out that a young person who has been traumatized, such as a teen mother or a young person damaged by rape or murder, will not be shocked by a sexually explicit young-adult novel. In his opinion, the critics of his novels are not trying to protect kids. Rather, they are protecting their opinions about what literature should be. He believes those critics are not really concerned about young people who face hardship every day, but are concerned about protecting privileged young people.

The purpose of Sherman's books is to give young people inspiration to cope with negative realities in their lives. Since many young people have suffered abuse, live with an alcoholic, or are alcoholics themselves, Sherman writes to let them know they are not alone. Since Sherman was sexually abused when he was young, he remembers what it was like to feel shame and loneliness. Sherman is also a recovering alcoholic who drank heavily when he was in school. He gave up drinking because he knew alcohol would eventually destroy his creativity. He made that choice, and he wants to help young people see that they can make positive choices too.

Sherman's popularity is evident by the mail he receives daily. Along with the typical fan letter, he also gets letters

SHERMAN ALEXIE QUOTES

- "If one reads enough books, one has a fighting chance. Or better, one's chances of survival increase with each book one reads."
- "The whole notion of reading a book is that it involves all of your senses."
- "The world, even the smallest parts of it, is filled with things you don't know."
- "Read. Read one thousand pages for every one page you write."
- "In most people's minds, American Indians only exist in the nineteenth century."
- "If you're good at it, and you love it, and it helps you navigate the river of the world, then it can't be wrong."
- "I realize now that the conditions that Indians are living in are the conditions that poor people everywhere are living in."

from kids who suffer from abuse and need someone they can talk to. According to Sherman, the kids who write those letters have lives darker than any he has ever written or read about.

Sherman refers to himself as a method writer. Just as a method actor prepares himself for a role in a movie, Sherman imagines he is the character he is writing about. He will spend many hours getting in touch with his character's emotions. It is a very physically and mentally exhausting process.

In addition to writing poetry and fiction, Sherman writes and directs films. He wrote the screenplay for the 1998 Hollywood movie *Smoke Signals*, which is the first commercially successful film directed and produced by Indians. All the actors in the movie were Indians, and the film was shown in major movie theaters across the country.

As if writing and directing movies wasn't enough, Sherman has put his great sense of humor to work in a stand-up comedy act. He describes his stand-up comedy as old-fashioned

Sherman Alexie on stage

storytelling. He points out that for many generations, it was tradition for Indians to stand up in front of the fire and tell stories. One time when Sherman got on stage and began talking, people laughed. At first he didn't know what was happening, but he soon realized people were enjoying themselves. Since then he has used his humor to rise above political, racial, geographic, and economic differences in his audiences.

Sherman spends a lot of time doing charitable work and speaking on college campuses. One piece of advice he gives future writers is to read as many books as possible. He reads an average of one book a day, and his private collection of books totals over five thousand.

Today, Sherman continues to write, speak to audiences, and play basketball. He and his wife, Diane Tomhave, who is of Hidatsa, Ho-Chunk, and Potawatomi heritage, live in Seattle, Washington, with their two sons.

Selected Works of Sherman Alexie
POETRY

"Postcards to Columbus," *American Diaspora: Poetry of Displacement*. University of Iowa Press, 2001.

"I Would Steal Horses," 1992.

"On the Amtrak from Boston to New York City," 1990.

FICTION AND POETRY COLLECTIONS

Face. Hanging Loose Press, 2009.

War Dances. Atlantic Monthly Press, 2009.

Flight. Black Cat, 2007.

The Absolutely True Diary of a Part-Time Indian. Little, Brown and Company, 2007.

Dangerous Astronomy. Limberlost, 2005.

Ten Little Indians. Grove Press, 2003.

One Stick Song. Hanging Loose Press, 2000.

The Toughest Indian in the World. Atlantic Monthly Press, 2000.

The Man Who Loves Salmon. Limberlost, 1998.

Water Flowing Home. Limberlost, 1996.

The Summer of Black Widows. Hanging Loose Press, 1996.

Indian Killer. Atlantic Monthly Press, 1996.

Reservation Blues. Atlantic Monthly Press, 1995.

Seven Mourning Songs for the Cedar Flute I Have Yet to Learn to Play. Whitman College Book Arts Lab, 1994.

Old Shirts and New Skins. American Indian Studies Center, 1993.

First Indian on the Moon. Hanging Loose Press, 1993.

The Lone Ranger and Tonto Fistfight in Heaven. Atlantic Monthly Press, 1993.

The Business of Fancydancing. Hanging Loose Press, 1992.

FILMS

49? Independent film, 2003.

The Business of Fancydancing. FallsApart Productions, 2002.

Smoke Signals. Miramax Films, 1998.

AWARDS AND HONORS

PEN/Faulkner Award, 2010.

Native Writers' Circle of the Americas Lifetime Achievement Award, 2010.

First American Puterbaugh Fellow, 2010.

California Young Reader Medal, 2010.

National Book Award for Young People's Literature, 2007.

New York Times Book Review Notable Children's Book, 2007.

New Yorker's 20 Writers for the 21st Century, 1999.

Before Columbus Foundation's American Book Award, 1996.

Granta magazine's Twenty Best Young American Novelists, 1996.

New York Times Notable Book, 1996.

National Endowment for the Arts Poetry Fellowship, 1992.

Louise Erdrich

Louise Erdrich was born on June 16, 1954, in Little Falls, Minnesota. She was the first of seven children and grew up in the small town of Wahpeton, North Dakota. Her mother, who is Ojibwe and French, was born on the Turtle Mountain Reservation, which is located five miles north of Wahpeton. Louise can trace her mother's family back to the time when Indians first came in contact with the French fur trappers. Her father's father came from a small town in Germany called Pforzheim. He moved to the United States shortly after World War I.

Louise's mother and father were teachers in a Bureau of Indian Affairs boarding school for Native American children. Education was also an important part of their family life. They brought their love of reading into their home and encouraged their children to read and write. Louise spent much of her youth reading books

Louise Erdrich

by her favorite authors, including Jane Austen, Willa Cather, George Eliot, William Faulkner, and Toni Morrison.

Her mother, always the teacher, designed flash cards to help her younger children learn to read. She attached them to household items, including the couch, television, and refrigerator. With her sewing machine, she made colorful paper books with zigzag-stitched bindings for her daughters. Louise and her sisters would write and illustrate stories in them.

Louise's parents had a large family and didn't have extra money to buy books. Instead they took their children on frequent trips to the library. Her father memorized and recited to his children the works of famous poets, such as Robert Frost, Henry Wadsworth Longfellow, and Alfred, Lord Tennyson. He paid his children a nickel for every poem they wrote or memorized.

Her parents could identify the birds and plants living around them. On hikes, they taught their children how to recognize various birds, plants, mushrooms, and the many varieties of apples grown on nearby farms.

Storytelling was another important part of life in the Erdrich family. People visited and told stories around the wood stove or fire, and Louise and all her siblings would listen. Her mother and grandparents spoke about life on the reservation during the Great Depression of the 1930s and the Ojibwe way of life. Her father told stories about his relatives and the towns where he grew up.

Because of the tales she heard as a child, Louise weaves both her Ojibwe and German heritage into her writing. In her work, she vividly describes the countryside that she knew as a child. When they were growing up, Louise and her siblings were taught that Native people protect their culture and the land. Her mother made sure her children were proud of who they were.

Louise attended a Catholic school in Wahpeton. Her grandfather, who was the tribal chairman of the Turtle Mountain Reservation, taught her about culture and religion. He practiced the traditional Ojibwe religion, but he was also a devout Catholic.

In 1972, after graduating from high school, eighteen-year-old Louise enrolled in Dartmouth College in Hanover, New Hampshire. She was a member of the college's first coeducational graduating class.

COEDUCATION

Coeducation is the term used when men and women attend the same college or university. Up until 1855 in the United States and 1880 in Canada, women were not even permitted to attend college. When they did enroll in a coeducational school, they often did not have the same rights or advantages as the male students. For example, some classes were not offered to women, and in some cases women could not be in the same classroom as men. In addition, music clubs and other extracurricular activities were often off limits to women. At one university, women had to be seated after the men; at another, women could not use the library if men were using it.

Title IX of the Education Amendments of 1972 guaranteed that no person in the United States could be denied an education on the basis of gender by a school receiving federal funds. After Title IX, college enrollment rates for women in the United States increased dramatically. By 2008 more women than men earned a doctorate degree in the United States.

Louise was very homesick during her time at college. She found herself living in a totally different environment than she was used to, and she was fifteen hundred miles from her family. To find comfort, she started writing about her home in a diary.

Because her family could not provide financial support, Louise had to work while attending college. Her experiences from a variety of jobs, including working on farms, in construction, and as a waitress, gave her a lot to write about in her diaries. It was also during her time at Dartmouth that Louise began writing poetry. Her poems were about her Ojibwe heritage, and in 1975 she was awarded the Academy of American Poets Prize.

Along with becoming a coeducational university the year Louise enrolled, Dartmouth also added a department of Native American studies and named anthropologist Michael Dorris chairperson. Louise was drawn to the new and exciting department, and she and Michael became close friends. However, after she graduated, they went their separate ways.

After college Louise served as a visiting poet and teacher for the North Dakota Council on the Arts. Following that, she was communications director and editor for the *Circle*, a newspaper sponsored by the Boston Indian Council. Later, she worked as a textbook writer for the Charles E. Merrill Publishing Company.

Louise decided to return to school after working at these various jobs. She enrolled at Johns Hopkins University in Baltimore, Maryland, and graduated in 1979 with a master's degree in creative writing. She wrote poetry for her course work and for her master's thesis. Some of these poems were included in her book *Jacklight*, which was published in 1984.

Louise returned to Dartmouth for a poetry reading and saw Michael again. They began dating and fell in love, but work-related requirements kept them apart. They stayed in contact by exchanging letters for one year, then they got together and were married in 1981. Michael had three adopted children he brought to the marriage, and over the course of their marriage he and Louise had three children of their own.

During the first year of their marriage, Louise and Michael worked together on writing projects. They conducted research together, developed plot lines and characters together, and discussed all aspects of a draft before submitting it to a publisher. Their work was published under both of their names. For a while, they cowrote romantic fiction to pay their bills. They used the pen name Milou North: "Mi" for Michael and "lou" for Louise. North referred to North Dakota, where they lived. One of their fiction pieces was published by *Redbook* magazine, but most were sold to publishers in Europe.

In 1982 Louise began writing on her own and received the Nelson Algren Short Story Award for "The World's Greatest Fisherman," which was one of two thousand entries for the award. She wrote the entire first draft in one day and completed the story in only two weeks. "The World's Greatest Fisherman" eventually became the first chapter of her first novel, *Love Medicine*, which was published in 1984.

Louise wrote *Love Medicine* when she was thirty years old. The novel was a huge success and won many awards, including the 1984 National Book Critics Circle Award for Fiction, the Sue Kaufman Prize for First Fiction, and the Virginia McCormick Scully Literary Award. The following year *Love Medicine* won the *Los Angeles Times* Book Prize for Fiction, the Before Columbus Foundation's American Book Award, and the Great Lakes Colleges Association New Writers Award.

Love Medicine is the first of four novels in a series that covers several generations of Ojibwe families living in Argus, North Dakota, between 1912 and the 1980s. In this first novel, seven characters from two families tell fourteen stories about themselves and their relationships. Readers, especially Native Americans, appreciate Louise's realistic portrayal of Native American life. The book has been translated into eighteen foreign languages and has enthusiastic followers through many mail-order book clubs.

Louise's second novel in the Argus series, *The Beet Queen*, was published in 1986. It begins in 1932, when three fatherless children are abandoned by their mother. The story continues over a forty-year period during which the children grow up and experience numerous misfortunes. *The Beet Queen* earned Louise glowing reviews, including this one from the *Los Angeles Times*: "Her prose spins and sparkles, and dances right on the heart."

Tracks, the third book in the Argus series, was published in 1988. This story takes place in North and South Dakota in the 1900s and explores the tension between Native American spirituality and Catholicism. *Publishers Weekly* called it a "beautifully fashioned, powerful novel."

In 1994 Louise published *The Bingo Palace*, the fourth and final novel in the Argus series, which intermingles people and stories from previous novels in the series. In all four books, Louise's research about the Ojibwe and North Dakota is evident in her powerful descriptions. *Library Journal* stresses this point in its review: "Erdrich's fourth novel is at once comic and moving, magical and realistic, and filled with evidence of her awesome descriptive powers."

Two years later, the novel *Tales of Burning Love* was released. The book received positive reviews from critics who praised the humor, compassion, and emotion that Louise brought to it. The story involves four women who become stranded in a blizzard while traveling together to attend the funeral of a man they had all been married to. The man's former wives compare their reasons for both marrying him and moving on.

Although Louise was experiencing success as an author, her personal life was riddled with misfortune and heartbreak. In 1991 Michael's oldest adopted son was struck by a car and died. The terrible ordeal caused Michael to drift into depression. In 1995 some of their children accused Michael of sexual abuse. The stress on their marriage became unbearable, and they separated later that year. Michael was drawn deeper and deeper into depression, and in 1997 he committed suicide.

In 1995, in the midst of this troubling time, Louise published *The Antelope Wife*. The novel examines love, family, and history among two Ojibwe families living in modern-day Minneapolis. One of the main characters is a husband whose wife leaves him, causing him to become depressed, drink heavily, and eventually commit suicide.

After this tragic time in her life, Louise continued to write. In 2003 she published the novel *Master Butcher's Singing Club.* The story takes place in North Dakota and interweaves the lives of a German World War I veteran, his wife, a group of traveling circus performers, and residents in small towns. The main character was based on Louise's grandmother, who performed in a show that traveled throughout Iowa. Louise discovered a photograph of her grandmother in an amazing pose, with a stack of chairs on her stomach and a man standing on his hands on the very top chair. Louise remembers her grandmother as a very strong and intelligent woman who did not have much formal education.

Another main character in *Master Butcher's Singing Club* is based on her grandfather, Ludwig Erdrich. Louise has a photograph of him that was taken when he was seventeen years old. His hair is carefully combed, and his clean white apron is gleaming. He became a master butcher and fought in World War I. He was decorated with the Iron Cross, a military award from the German army. Even though he served his country and won a prestigious military decoration, her grandfather was disgusted with war. He decided to go to America and start a new life, so he left Germany in 1920.

From the time she was a child, Louise has always written in a diary or journal. Her first one was a little book with a gold key to lock it. She has kept all her diaries, and whenever she picks one up to read, she is always surprised. Sometimes she comes across entries she can use in one of her poems or novels.

Journal writing is still important to Louise. It is how she stores bits of knowledge that she may someday use in one of her works. She also collects books about bizarre and supernatural experiences and jots down notes about them in her journals.

In 1999 Louise and her three youngest children relocated to Minneapolis, Minnesota, to be closer to her parents. One year later, as Louise and her daughters walked by a blackened storefront window in their quiet Minneapolis neighborhood, they began fantasizing about opening a bookstore, complete with a bookstore cat like one they had seen in a Hollywood movie. When the space came up for lease, Louise and her sister Heidi Erdrich, a poet, decided to open Birchbark Books.

The bookstore staff works hard to find and stock the very best children's books, especially those with a special emphasis on Native American life. In addition to books, the store stocks quillwork, traditional basketry, silverwork, unusual dream catchers, and Native American paintings. A very popular item is a pair of earrings just like Louise's lucky silver feather earrings. A handmade wooden canoe hangs from the ceiling, and the bookstore has some enticing nooks for children, such as a tiny birchbark loft and a "hobbit hole" where they can play and read.

One installation that makes Birchbark Books different from most bookstores is a Roman Catholic confessional that Louise rescued from the junk pile. Beautiful dream catchers dangle from the corners of the confessional, adding to its uniqueness.

The same year that Louise and her sister opened their bookstore, Louise released a children's book called *The Birchbark House.* In this wonderful story, Louise takes readers back in time to 1847. The setting is an island in Lake Superior. The story involves a seven-year-old Ojibwe girl named Omakayas. Young readers are fascinated as Omakayas struggles and triumphs through a full cycle of seasons, sharing her secrets, joys, and fears.

Louise says she enjoys writing Native American literature because it is about coming home and returning to the land, the language, and the love of ancient traditions. Because American Indian languages are in danger of becoming extinct, Louise is deeply involved in learning the Ojibwe language and finding out more about her Ojibwe roots. In her continued effort to reclaim the Ojibwe language, she has replaced English words in her children's picture books with Ojibwe words.

Louise Erdrich at Dartmouth commencement

Louise survived the early days of intense public interest in her work, life, and history. Today she lives in a quiet Minneapolis neighborhood that is part of a vibrant urban American Indian community. Her fans love her and eagerly look forward to her next book. Despite her continued success and having even been named one of *People* magazine's most beautiful people, she remains modest, describing herself as a woman from a small Midwestern small town who loves words and gets more pleasure from walking in the woods than going on a cross-country book tour.

Selected Works of Louise Erdrich

NOVELS

Shadow Tag. Harper, 2010.

The Plague of Doves. HarperCollins, 2008.

The Painted Drum. HarperCollins, 2005.

Four Souls. HarperCollins, 2004.

The Master Butcher's Singing Club. HarperCollins, 2003.

The Last Report on the Miracles at Little No Horse. HarperCollins, 2001.

The Antelope Wife. HarperFlamingo, 1998.

Tales of Burning Love. HarperCollins, 1996.

The Bingo Palace. HarperCollins, 1994.

The Crown of Columbus (with Michael Dorris). HarperCollins, 1991.

Tracks. Henry Holt, 1988.

The Beet Queen. Holt, 1986.

Love Medicine. Holt, 1984.

SHORT STORIES

The Red Convertible: Collected and New Stories 1978–2008. HarperCollins, 2009.

CHILDREN'S BOOKS

The Porcupine Year. HarperCollins, 2008.

The Game of Silence. HarperCollins, 2005.

The Range Eternal. Hyperion Books for Children, 2002.

The Birchbark House. Hyperion Books for Children, 1999.

Grandmother's Pigeon. Hyperion Books for Children, 1996.

POETRY COLLECTIONS

Original Fire: Selected and New Poems. HarperCollins, 2003.

Baptism of Desire: Poems. Harper & Row, 1989.

Jacklight. Holt, 1984.

NONFICTION

Books and Islands in Ojibwe Country. National Geographic Society, 2003.

The Blue Jay's Dance: A Birth Year. HarperCollins, 1995.

Route Two (with Michael Dorris). Lord John Press, 1991.

AWARDS AND HONORS

Dartmouth College Honorary Doctor of Letters, 2009.

Scott O'Dell Award for Historical Fiction, 2006.

Associate Poet Laureate of North Dakota, 2005.

Native Writers' Circle of the Americas Lifetime Achievement Award, 2000.

World Fantasy Award, 1999.

O. Henry Award, 1987.

Before Columbus Foundation's American Book Award, 1985.

Great Lakes Colleges Association New Writers Award, 1985.

Guggenheim Fellowship, 1985.

Los Angeles Times Book Prize for Fiction, 1985.

National Book Critics Circle Award for Fiction, 1984.

Sue Kaufman Prize for First Fiction, 1984.

Virginia McCormick Scully Award, 1984.

Pushcart Prize in Poetry, 1983.

Nelson Algren Short Story Award, 1982.

Academy of American Poets Prize, 1975.

Joseph Boyden

Joe Boyden was born on October 31, 1966, into an Irish Catholic family in Willowdale, a suburb of Toronto, Ontario. He was one of eleven children. His father was a physician, and Joe and most of his siblings were born late in his father's life. Joe tells people his father was older than most of his friends' grandfathers; in fact, he delivered many of Joe's schoolmates' parents.

Joe's ancestry is part Ojibwe with Irish and Scottish mixed in, but his Ojibwe roots are very important to Joe. His family's mixed heritage is evident in the differences between his father and uncle. Joe's father, Raymond Wilfrid Boyden, had light features and blue eyes, and his father's older brother, Erl, had dark features.

Joseph Boyden

In addition to their physical differences, the brothers also had very different lifestyles. Joe's father was a doctor who had served in the military and became a war hero. He and his family lived in the city. In contrast, Erl chose a more traditional Native American way of life. He lived in the woods of northern Ontario in the summer and traveled in the winter.

In 1945, after World War II had ended, Joe's father was invited to Buckingham Palace by King George VI, who awarded him the Distinguished Service Order. This honor made him a very highly decorated medical officer.

Joe was a typical little boy who grew up hearing many tales about his family and their history. The stories were about his father's war exploits and his Uncle Erl's Ojibwe ways.

Like most kids, Joe loved to play outdoors. He and his many siblings played lots of games, including cowboys and Indians. They also liked to roughhouse in the schoolyard next door and chase around the goats his father accepted in exchange for the medical services he gave to some of his patients.

Joe has fond memories of the trips he and his family took with his father. During the summer or whenever the kids were out of school for more than a few days, Joe's father closed his practice and traveled with his family to Georgian Bay in Ontario. His father loved the land and animals, and he passed that love and respect for the natural world on to his close-knit family. Joe's mother also has a love for that area. After she retired from teaching, she moved to Georgian Bay and has lived there for over twenty years. Joe's connection to Georgian Bay remains strong, and memories about his family's trips have had a great influence on his writing.

Joe learned to read early and was an avid reader. At age six, he read his way through the *Encyclopedia Britannica*. When he found and read S. E. Hinton's novel *The Outsiders*, he started thinking about a career in writing. In addition to reading, he loved to hear stories about his father, who died when Joe was only eight years old. It was hard for Joe to lose his father, and he felt he was always looking for him and wondering about him. His loss, along with all he had heard about his father's military career, influenced Joe's writing.

During his teens, Joe developed some patterns that reflected his Uncle Erl's lifestyle. Joe was adventurous and loved being on the road. At age sixteen, he began traveling alone during the summer. He developed many friendships, especially in South Carolina and Louisiana. Joe became a roadie for a rock-and-roll band and traveled throughout the United States and Canada with them. But he knew how important his schooling was, so he always returned home in the fall.

So that he could afford to travel, Joe had to work many different jobs, including gravedigger and groundskeeper at a cemetery. He also tutored students. He worked through the school year and after he took his last examination of the semester, he hit the road again. He traveled by Greyhound bus, hitchhiked, or rode his motorcycle.

Joe eventually earned a bachelor of arts in creative writing from York University in Toronto. During his travels in the United States he developed an interest in the American South, so he decided to attend the University of New Orleans in Louisiana, where he earned his master of fine arts in creative writing. It is also where he met his wife, Amanda, who is a trapeze artist, contortionist, and writer.

After they were married the couple moved to Ontario, where Joe accepted a job as professor of Aboriginal programs at Northern College in northeastern Ontario. His job entailed traveling by bush plane, helicopter, snowmobile, or canoe up and down the west coast of Hudson Bay. When he was not working, he enjoyed hunting moose and caribou and journeying by snowmobile into the wilderness of the bay area.

While working and traveling with his job at Northern College, Joe was introduced to the Mushkegowuk Cree, the northern cousins of the Ojibwe. He taught a communications course and general arts and sciences to students who were trying to get a college degree. All of his students were Native Americans. For Joe, this teaching job was a life-changing experience.

It was during his time teaching and getting to personally know Aboriginal people that he began writing. Joe's first book, a collection of short stories about Native people titled *Born with a Tooth*, was published in 2000. But it was his first novel, *Three Day Road*, that gained Joe instant popularity. The book became an immediate success, earning praise such as the following from readers: "highly captivating," "a poignant tale of brutality and survival," and "a compelling read, beautifully told and timeless in its lessons." The novel has been translated into fifteen languages and has been published in over fifty countries.

Joe drew a large part of *Three Day Road* from his family's stories. One of the characters is based on two individuals: his maternal grandfather, who was a motorcycle dispatch rider in World War I and was blinded in one eye on the last day of the war, and Francis Pegahmagabow, a famous Ojibwe sharpshooter and legendary World War I sniper.

Three Day Road tells the tale of two young Cree men, Xavier Bird and Elijah Weesageechak (also known as Whiskeyjack) who volunteer for the war and become snipers. Because both Xavier and Elijah are sharpshooters who learned hunting in the forests of Hudson Bay, they are naturals as snipers. They share qualities that enhance this skill: both can lie still for hours and sense a human presence without actually seeing anyone, and both move quietly, especially when they are allowed to wear their moccasins. However, a significant difference distinguishes one from the other: while one thrives on

FRANCIS PEGAHMAGABOW

Francis Pegahmagabow was an expert Métis scout and marksman. He put his skills to use during World War I and was awarded military honors three times for his bravery. He is considered one of the war's most effective snipers. Later in life, he served as chief and a counselor for the Wasauksing First Nation and as an activist and leader for several First Nations organizations.

hunting men, the other is unhappy about what he considers senseless killing.

No one has ever talked about World War I like Joe does in *Three Day Road*, where he examines the cultural conflicts that arose between the whites and Native Americans. In fact, the experiences of the Native men who served are missing from many stories about both World Wars, for which a great number of Native men volunteered. Their stories are not known, and Joe feels they were not recognized for their accomplishments.

Joseph Boyden at a book signing

Joe's second novel, *Through Black Spruce*, brings back the character Will Bird from *Three Day Road*. The book follows the life of Will's niece Annie Bird, a Moosonee Cree woman. Joe takes his reader on a journey from the bush country of Ontario to the grungy clubs of Manhattan. Annie returns from her own life journey to sit beside Will's hospital bed as he lies in a coma. Both have suffered heartbreak, but together they find quiet unity.

Hunting is significant in both of Joe's novels. While hunting as a child, Joe was told to "Just sit, wait, and be patient." These are skills he continues to use today. His writing underscores how important it is to pass on traditional hunting skills to children. Hunting continues to be a big part of Joe's life, and he hunts with his son, Jacob, and brothers to fill up the freezer for winter. He goes to a hunting camp near Moosonee, Ontario, and also likes to spend some time in northern Ontario. His family's trips to the bush country were an important part of his early life, and similar trips are important to him as an adult. These visits help him remain close to his roots, and First Nations experiences are what he feels compelled to write about.

Currently, Joe and his wife are both writers in residence at the University of New Orleans. He inspires young writers by using himself as an example. When he was teaching while writing a novel, he found he had to write early in the morning, which was the only time he felt completely committed to writing. After working all day, he didn't feel like writing at night. He created a schedule for himself, and got up early every morning to write. By talking with his students about his regimen, he showed how writing could fit into really busy lives.

Joe goes to northern Ontario to revive his spirit. There he finds beauty along with a calmness that contrasts with his busy life back in New Orleans. When he returns to the United States, he looks at Canada with a clear perspective. The distance between his adopted home and his homeland helps him maintain a fresh point of view about Canada. He feels that his emotional attachment to Canada, as well as the physical differences between the United States and Canada that he writes about, enhance his work.

Joe says he sees a parallel between the Aboriginal people in northern Ontario and people who live in New Orleans. In both places he finds a similar love of life, laughter, and enjoyment. He uses these themes in his stories to create new perspectives about First Nations people. He acknowledges that violence, drug and alcohol abuse, and poverty exist on reservations, but he also points out that many helpful programs are available for people who are dealing with these issues. Instead of focusing on the negative aspects of Native life, he focuses on the beauty of the land and the beauty of the people.

At times it may seem that Joe is two different people: an Ojibwe in northern Canada and a white man in the southern

United States. He also seems to have inherited a combination of traits from his Irish-Ojibwe heritage, including a sense of responsibility and a yearning to travel. At heart, he's a Canadian in America who is grounded by history and inspired by legend.

Selected Works of Joseph Boyden

NOVELS

Through Black Spruce. Viking, 2009.

Three Day Road. Viking, 2005.

SHORT STORIES

Born with a Tooth. Cormorant Books, 2001.

NONFICTION

Extraordinary Canadians: Louis Riel and Gabriel Dumont. Penguin Canada, 2010.

From Mushkegowuk to New Orleans: A Mixed Blood Highway. NeWest Press, 2008.

AWARDS AND HONORS

Amazon.ca/Books in Canada First Novel Award, 2005.

Governor General's Literary Award, 2005.

McNally Robinson Aboriginal Book of the Year Award, 2005.

Rogers Writers' Trust Fiction Prize, 2005.

N. Scott Momaday

avarre Scott Momaday, who uses his middle name, is credited for the rebirth of American Indian literature. Known as the dean of American Indian writers, he published his first novel, *House Made of Dawn,* in 1969. The book brought Native American literature to the attention of Americans from all walks of life and was awarded the Pulitzer Prize for Fiction the same year it was published. He is the only Native American to have been awarded this prize. Before Scott wrote *House Made of Dawn,* only six American Indian writers had published a total of nine novels. By the early 1990s more than thirty Indians had published novels.

N. Scott Momaday

Scott's novel began as a series of poems, which he rewrote as a series of stories and finally as a novel. The novel mixes real-life happenings with fiction, and the characters are based on the people of the Pueblo tribe in Jemez, New Mexico, where Scott lived for a time.

The book's main character is Abel, who came home to the Pueblo reservation after serving as a soldier in World War II. The day he returned, Abel was so drunk when he got off the train, he didn't recognize his own grandfather. As the story progresses, Abel's life only gets worse. In a drunken rage he kills another Indian and goes to prison. When he gets out of prison, he has a problem holding a job. Ultimately, he returns to the reservation to care for his dying grandfather.

Abel's behavior is a composite of the conduct Scott witnessed among the young Indian men he lived with at the Pueblo. After their return from the war, some of them died violent deaths. Many of their problems were caused by alcohol and the inability to readapt to reservation life after being out in the world. But these problems were not limited to the reservation; other American Indians who entered relocation programs and moved to major cities after the war also had a hard time adjusting and turned to alcohol.

Scott was born at Kiowa Indian Hospital in Comanche County, Oklahoma, on February 27, 1934. His father, Alfred, was a full-blooded Kiowa Indian who was born and raised on the Kiowa reservation in Oklahoma. The Kiowa pronunciation of Momaday is "Mammedaty." Scott's mother is part Cherokee and also has English, French, and Irish heritage. Both parents spent most of their lives teaching on reservations. Scott's father was an accomplished draftsman and painter, and his mother wrote children's books.

For the first year of his life, Scott lived with his grandmother on the Kiowa reservation in Oklahoma. The entire country was experiencing the Great Depression, and jobs were hard to come by. When Scott was one year old, his parents moved their small family in an attempt to find work. First they went to Arizona, then back to Oklahoma, and finally to Gallup, New Mexico, where they were employed as teachers at schools run by the Bureau of Indian Affairs. Because his parents frequently moved from state to state, Scott attended many different schools and became familiar with the Apache, Navajo, and Pueblo cultures. As a child he heard adults speak the Kiowa language, but he never learned it. As a result he was often the only student in his class who spoke unbroken English.

THE GREAT DEPRESSION

The Great Depression was one of the most severe economic depressions the United States has ever experienced. It began in 1929 following the collapse of the New York Stock Exchange. International trade as well as domestic manufacturing decreased. People working in rural America lost income when crop prices fell by 60 percent. The entire country experienced high unemployment rates. America's economy finally began to recover when factories opened to support the war effort after the United States entered World War II in 1941.

On December 7, 1941, when Scott was only seven years old, the Japanese bombed Pearl Harbor, Hawaii. In response, the United States immediately entered World War II and began sending soldiers to fight against Japan, Germany, and Italy. To support the war effort, Scott's parents quit teaching at the reservation schools. The family moved to Hobbs, New Mexico, where his father worked for oil companies that supplied the US military with fuel and his mother worked on the army base.

Even though his parents worked for the war effort, they encountered many acts of racism while living in Hobbs. They decided to move to Jemez Pueblo, where Scott's mother went back to teaching. She agreed to take the job only if Scott's father could join her, which he did. They became the only two teachers at a day school, and they remained there for the next twenty-five years. Scott's father was the principal, and his mother was the teacher. She taught grades one through three, and he taught grades four through six.

When Scott was about twelve, after the family moved to Jemez Pueblo, his parents gave him a small strawberry roan quarter horse that could run very quickly. The horse's name was Pecos. During the next few years, Scott became a pretty good rider and he entered Pecos in races, which Pecos usually won.

As a little boy, Scott happened to come across a book by Will James titled *Smokey the Cowhorse.* He fell in love with James' books about cowboys and horses, and he read every one that he could get his hands on. When he rode Pecos, he would pretend he was riding the range just like the characters in the books.

Scott attended four different high schools. At one time he traveled twenty-eight miles one way by bus to attend school. During his sophomore year, he lived in the home of an elderly German couple in Albuquerque, New Mexico. Because Scott had been to so many different schools in three years, he was worried that he was not adequately prepared for college. He discussed his worries with his parents, and they decided he should spend his senior year at a prep school.

Scott's mother grew up in Kentucky, so Scott had an interest in the history of the southern states. He sent for catalogs from a number of schools in the South and decided on Augusta Military Academy in Fort Defiance, Virginia. He enjoyed his year at the academy and graduated in 1952.

Scott spent his undergraduate years at the University of New Mexico, where he earned a bachelor's degree in political science. While he was at the university, he began writing poetry. He had not written anything before that, although while he was at the military academy he won third place in a public speaking contest held in Baltimore, Maryland.

After completing his bachelor's degree, Scott enrolled at the University of Virginia School of Law for a short time. At the university, he met writer in residence William Faulkner, author of the classic novel *The Sound and the Fury.* Faulkner had a big influence on Scott. In fact, Scott based one of his poems on Faulkner's short story "The Bear."

Scott decided to leave law school and took a job teaching seventh through twelfth grades on the Jicarilla Apache Res-

WILLIAM FAULKNER

William Faulkner was born in Mississippi in 1897. He is known as one of America's greatest writers of Southern literature, and most of his stories are based on his childhood home. His short story "The Bear" is considered one of the best short stories written in the twentieth century.

ervation in Dulce, New Mexico. Although he enjoyed working with kids and teaching for a living, he didn't want to give up writing. Ever since he was a child listening to the stories his parents told, he knew he wanted to be a writer. His father told Kiowa stories, and his mother, who was a writer, always encouraged him to write.

Mostly because of his mother's support, Scott applied for a Stegner Fellowship for creative writing at Stanford University in California. To his surprise, he was granted the fellowship. Scott took a leave of absence from teaching and moved to California, with a plan to return to the reservation after completing his studies. Instead, he ended up staying in California for twenty years. Entering the creative writing program at Stanford was an important turning point in his life.

Because Scott was the only poet awarded the Stegner Fellowship that year, Yvor Winters, an American poet in residence at Stanford, became Scott's tutor. Under Winters' direction, Scott earned a master's degree in English, followed by a doctorate degree in English literature. His degrees made him overqualified to teach at the school in New Mexico, so he decided to accept a teaching position at the University of California at Santa Barbara.

While teaching in Santa Barbara, he designed a course in American Indian studies. Since he had a great interest in the

Native American oral tradition, he developed a course to study Native oral tradition stories and songs. He taught students how Native stories and songs are formed and composed and how they compare to English poetry. He also taught the course for many years at Stanford University and the University of California at Berkeley. Later he became a visiting professor at Columbia University in New York City and at Princeton University in New Jersey.

In the 1970s Scott spent some time as a professor of American literature in Moscow, in what was then the Soviet Union. It was there that Scott became interested in drawing and painting. His father was a painter, and although Scott used to watch him paint, he had never been inclined to become a painter himself. He found he had talent, however, and both he and his father have done illustrations for Scott's books. In addition, Scott's artwork has been exhibited throughout the United States.

N. Scott Momaday

Scott believes there is a connection between painting and writing, but he treats each subject differently. He doesn't have to concentrate as hard when he paints, so he can listen to music or a ball game at the same time. However, when he writes he has to concentrate entirely on what he is writing. He believes that writing poetry is extremely important, and he would rather be a poet than a novelist.

Scott has won numerous awards. In 1992 he was awarded the Lifetime Achievement Award from the Native Writers' Circle of the Americas, and in 2007 president George W. Bush awarded him the National Medal of Arts. In 2010 the University of Chicago honored Scott with an honorary doctor of humane letters. He holds twelve honorary degrees from a number of American universities, including Yale University.

Scott was featured in the Ken Burns television documentary *The West*, where he talked about Kiowa history and legend. He also appeared in a PBS documentary about the Battle of Little Bighorn.

Today N. Scott Momaday can be found managing the Rainy Mountain Foundation and the Buffalo Trust, a nonprofit organization working to preserve Native cultures. In his leisure time, he paints in watercolors.

Selected Works of N. Scott Momaday

NOVELS

The Ancient Child. Doubleday, 1989.

House Made of Dawn. Harper, 1968.

NONFICTION

The Way to Rainy Mountain (illustrated by his father, Alfred Momaday). University of New Mexico Press, 1969.

PLAYS

Three Plays. University of Oklahoma Press, 2007.

AUTOBIOGRAPHY

The Names: A Memoir. Harper & Row, 1976.

SHORT STORIES AND POEMS

In the Bear's House. St. Martin's Press, 1999.

The Man Made of Words: Essays, Stories, Passages. St. Martin's Press, 1997.

Circle of Wonder: A Native American Christmas Story. Clear Light Publishers, 1993.

In the Presence of the Sun: Stories and Poems, 1961–1991. St. Martin's Press, 1992.

The Gourd Dancer: Poems. Harper & Row, 1976.

Angle of Geese and Other Poems. D. R. Godine, 1974.

The Journey of Tai-me. University of California, 1967.

AWARDS AND HONORS

Oklahoma Centennial Poet Laureate, July 12, 2007, to January 1, 2009.

National Medal of Arts, 2007.

Native Writers' Circle of the Americas Lifetime Achievement Award, 1992.

National Institute of Arts and Letters Award, 1970.

Pulitzer Prize for Fiction, 1969.

Guggenheim Fellowship, 1966.

Academy of American Poets Prize, 1962.

Stanford University Stegner Fellowship, 1958.

Marilyn Dumont

Marilyn Dumont, who has Cree and Métis ancestry, was born in 1955 in the tiny town of Olds in the province of Alberta, Canada. When she was growing up, her family spoke English, so Marilyn and her siblings never learned Cree. However, when something important happened, especially something the kids should not hear about, her mom and dad spoke Cree.

Marilyn's childhood was not always easy because her father's alcohol abuse created problems in her family. Her mother never drank, but her father was a binge drinker who didn't stop until he was drunk. Because of their father's drinking, Marilyn and the other children were concerned that their parents would not stay together, but they did for fifty years. As time went on, they had fewer differences and her father's alcohol abuse became less of a problem. Marilyn explains, "My family experience, like most, is filled with love, loyalty, fear, joy, terror, compassion, jealousy, and tenderness; somehow we survive our families and sometimes we thrive."

Marilyn Dumont

When Marilyn was very young, her family lived in a logging camp. She enjoyed running and playing with her brothers, sisters, and the horses that were used for pulling skids of logs. When she was three years old, she was involved in an unfortunate accident that could have been much worse. Her brother Danny, who was five or six at the time, accidently chopped off the little finger on her left hand, and she almost lost the two fingers next to it as well. Danny was so upset, he ran away from home and was gone for three days. Later in life, Marilyn drew from the incident when she wrote "The Sky is Promising," a poem that appears in her collection *A Really Good Brown Girl*. In the poem she asks her brother Danny to come home.

When she was old enough to attend school, Marilyn had to live in town with her older brother and sister. She hated school and skipped it every chance she could get. Her brother and sister got upset with her, but she was hard to discipline. She continued to skip school fairly regularly and stayed home to play with a preschool-age friend who lived down the street or just watch movies on television.

Music was part of Marilyn's family life when she was growing up. The family got together to sing and dance, which Marilyn loved to do. She sang in the church choir and dreamed of being a singer and a dancer when she grew up. One of her brothers sang and played guitar.

When she was in the fourth grade, Marilyn read a poem to her classmates that she had written. She had never read anything in front of her class before. "I was terrified," she recalls, "but I really liked it." By the time she was in tenth grade, she was enjoying poetry more and more. When her teacher recited *The Rime of the Ancient Mariner*, a poem written in 1798 by the English poet Samuel Taylor Coleridge, Marilyn loved it and knew she was really hooked on poetry.

It wasn't until 1985 that Marilyn began to seriously think about becoming a professional writer. She was in her early thirties and recently separated from her husband of thirteen years, but she was optimistic. She viewed the world as a field of opportunities just waiting for her, and she decided to enroll in a noncredit poetry writing course at the Banff Centre Writing Studio. Her teacher encouraged her to send her poems to different magazines, and Marilyn was pleasantly surprised when two of her poems were accepted. She continued to submit poems and even started to wonder if she might be able to put together an entire collection.

One day while she was chatting with a fellow writer, Marilyn told him about her poems. He looked at her manuscript and suggested that she submit it to Brick Books. She didn't know at the time that he was the editor of Brick Books. About six to eight months after she submitted her poems, the publisher decided to publish her book. Marilyn waited patiently for two years, and in 1996 her first collection of poems, titled *A Really Good Brown Girl*, was released.

Written for grades nine to twelve, *A Really Good Brown Girl* was a huge success. It was awarded the 1997 Gerald Lampert Memorial Award presented by the League of Canadian Poets. It is now in its twelfth printing and is used as a textbook in twenty-three learning institutions in Canada and the United States.

A Really Good Brown Girl is Marilyn's autobiography. She writes about the realities of being a Métis in Canadian society. In one of the poems, "The Red and White," she refers to "do-gooders" who are continually trying to make brown children into white children. She also writes about the double life she lived by keeping her Aboriginal and white worlds separate. She explains how she adapted to fit in and be accepted in white society, how she became invisible on her first day of school, and how she survived by watching and following the other students. Over time, school became more manageable. By the time Marilyn was in fifth grade, she was declared the most improved student.

Marilyn's poems give a voice to her ancestors' struggles. The limitations placed on Native people by white society and by rivalries within Aboriginal society are recurring themes in her poems. Her "race," as she puts it, has been very important to her writing. In all her poetry she is honest and direct, but her sense of humor also comes through.

Marilyn is quick to point out that even though her writing contains much about her childhood, it is also creative and original. She transforms history into story and fact into fiction. She writes about the shame of growing up Métis, as well as the strength and humor demonstrated by the women of her community, especially her mother.

There is a photo in *A Really Good Brown Girl* of a young Marilyn and her mother, and Marilyn has received numerous questions about it. She explains that it was taken in the 1960s by someone who was trying to make money on the

Marilyn Dumont, as a child, with her mother

street by taking a picture and then selling it to the subject. Marilyn finds significance in the photo and notes how large her mother looked and how small she looked: "It gives me a sense that she was there protecting me, and how innocent I look, and how vulnerable to shame we are as children."

Marilyn remembers her mother's great sense of humor, which was mostly sarcastic. She points out that in a crowd of Native people, the women still make fun of the men in a sarcastic way. "I think it's cultural, the joking, the kind of competition between men and women about who can be the wittiest and undercut the other ones," she says.

Marilyn loves to experiment with the form poetry can take. She incorporates Cree words, and she also mixes poetry and prose together. She likes to say she has discovered a third language that allows her poetry to explore all aspects of her personal, family, and cultural history. Marilyn finds inspiration to write poetry in many different sources, such as a newspaper headline, a poetry reading, music, or even just a memory. Sometimes she experiences what is called "writer's block," which is when a writer can't think of anything to write about. When this happens, she reads poetry and books on how to write.

Even though she is the youngest, her family members all come to Marilyn for stories. Still, she is not sure if any of them have ever read her published poems. She says it can be a little scary not knowing what they think of her work, but she has never asked any of them for their opinion.

Marilyn's book *A Really Good Brown Girl* brought her some degree of celebrity and numerous positive reviews, but she was disappointed by how the publisher promoted her work. Instead of focusing on her writing, the publisher promoted her as a descendant of Gabriel Dumont, who was a famous leader of the Métis people of western Canada in the mid-1800s. Marilyn says, "My first book launched me into the publishing world, and I was mostly prepared, but I later recognized that the book marketing world will do whatever it needs to attract attention to its product." Since then, Marilyn has worked hard to promote herself as a writer first, and a descendant of a great man, second.

Readers are drawn to Marilyn's poetry for many reasons, but mostly because it appeals to their emotions and their senses. People also read her poetry because of how it intersects with their own spiritual or political views. Like other art forms, poetry can influence readers to think beyond their own beliefs and consider alternative possibilities.

Marilyn has been inspired by a number of female poets. "Sharon Olds is someone who really influenced me," she says. "I guess because of the courage with which she was willing to look at things in her own family and her own psyche."

"Once you've read so much poetry, you want to find some new voices," says Marilyn. "Basically, with any woman poet that I don't know, I'll pick up and look through her work. I find that I always want to learn more."

GABRIEL DUMONT

Gabriel Dumont is best known as the man who led the small Métis army during the North-West Rebellion of 1885. The Métis were protesting the takeover of Batoche, a settlement they established in Saskatchewan in 1872. The government was going to move the Métis to make room for the influx of white settlers, so Dumont led a small band of three hundred Métis and other Indians against a force of eight hundred government troops. After four days of fierce fighting, Dumont's army was forced to surrender. Dumont escaped to the Montana Territory, where he surrendered to the US Cavalry. The US government determined that he was a political refugee, and he was released. In 1886 Dumont was granted amnesty by the Canadian government. In 1893 he returned to his beloved Canada, where he once again lived as a farmer, hunter, and trapper.

One of Marilyn's all-time favorite books is *The Grapes of Wrath*, a classic by John Steinbeck. She says, "I could identify with the poverty and desperation of the characters when I was age ten." Another favorite book is *She Had Some Horses* by Joy Harjo: "She showed me how to write about the beauty of Aboriginal belief and traditions."

Marilyn also has other interests, including quilting, beading, sewing, and making collages. She sometimes works on a single project for months and months. She finds it ironic that she now enjoys beadwork, because her mother did beadwork when Marilyn was a child, and she had no interest in it then.

Marilyn's formal education started with a single noncredit writing class, but she persevered and received a bachelor of arts from the University of Alberta followed by a master of fine arts in creative writing from the University of British Columbia. She has held the position of writer in residence at Grant MacEwan College and the University of Alberta, which are both in Edmonton, and the University of Toronto and the University of Windsor, which are both in Ontario. In addition, she has taught creative writing at Simon Fraser University and Kwantlen Polytechnic University, which are both in British Columbia.

Today, Marilyn lives in Edmonton, Alberta, and she teaches creative writing at Athabasca University. She is working on a collection of poetry that focuses on Gabriel Dumont.

What advice does Marilyn give to young people who are pursuing a writing career? She says, "It's important to research your own cultural group. Find out what you can. It's important to know those things."

Selected Works of Marilyn Dumont

POETRY

"The Sound of One Hand Drumming." *Women & Environments International Magazine,* 2002.

ANTHOLOGY

Initiations: A Selection of Young Native Writings. Theytus Books, 2007.

POETRY COLLECTIONS

That Tongued Belonging. Kegedonce Press, 2007.

Green Girl Dreams Mountains. Oolichan Books, 2001.

A Really Good Brown Girl. Brick Books, 1996.

Numerous poems from Marilyn Dumont's collections are included in elementary, secondary, and postsecondary textbooks and are also in other anthologies.

AWARDS AND HONORS

McNally Robinson Aboriginal Book of the Year Award, 2007.

Stephan G. Stephansson Award for Poetry, 2002.

Alberta Book Award for Poetry, 2001.

Gerald Lampert Memorial Award, 1997.

Tomson Highway

Tomson Highway is a full-blooded Cree Indian, author, playwright, and concert pianist. On October 27, 1993, he became the first Aboriginal writer to be inducted into the Order of Canada, the nation's highest civilian honor, for his contribution to preserving Canadian Native heritage.

Tomson was born on December 6, 1951, in a tent pitched in a snowbank near Maria Lake in northern Manitoba, Canada. He grew up in the beautiful outdoors of subarctic Canada, an unpopulated area with hundreds of lakes, abundant pine and spruce forests, and large herds of caribou.

Tomson is the eleventh of twelve children, seven girls and five boys. His father, Joe, was an expert fisherman, hunter,

Tomson Highway

and world champion sled dog racer. His mother, Pelagie, was a bead worker and quilt maker. When he was growing up, Tomson's family had no access to books, television, or radio. For entertainment, his parents told the children stories. Tomson fell in love with the Cree Indian tradition of oral storytelling. His parents told their stories in the Cree language, which was the only language spoken in his family. As a result, Tomson did not speak English correctly until he became a teenager.

Music was an important part of Tomson's family life. His father was an accordion player, and his grandfather was known far and wide as an accomplished fiddle player. Many members of the Highway family played guitar and sang. Tomson learned to play the piano as a young boy.

Tomson and his brothers grew up helping their father trap animals and fish. Their father owned five fishing and trapping camps. Every camp had a cabin and an icehouse that his father built with his own hands, two canoes, traps, and fishing nets. The family moved from camp to camp, and enough food was stored at each camp to last the family an entire summer.

Trapping and fishing was a hard life for a youngster, but Tomson believes his early childhood was special and magical. In fact, his first diaper was made from rabbit skin. He enjoyed the dogs and dog sledding, hunting caribou, and setting traps.

When Tomson was six years old, he and his brother René were taken from their family and placed in the Guy Hill Indian Residential School, a Roman Catholic school in The Pas, a small town near The Pas Indian Reserve in Manitoba. Racism was common in The Pas. Natives were not allowed to sit in the same section as white people in the movie theater, and were arrested much more frequently than white people.

At Guy Hill School, the students were pressured to give up their Native way of life and adopt the white man's ways. Tomson was abused by priests at the school, and at age fifteen he left to attend Churchill High School in Winnipeg, Canada, where he lived with white families. He was allowed to go home for two months each year. Being away from his parents for all those years was upsetting for Tomson. However, he found some comfort at Churchill, where he was given the opportunity to pursue his dream of becoming a concert pianist.

After graduating from high school in 1970, Tomson spent two years studying piano at the University of Manitoba

---

JAMES REANEY

James Reaney was a Canadian poet, playwright, professor, and librettist. A librettist writes the words that accompany an extended musical work, such as an opera. Reaney was very influential and won awards for both his poetry and drama. He was awarded the Canadian Governor General's Award three times.

Faculty of Music. Then he moved to London, England, to study piano with Canadian music specialist William Aide. When he returned to Canada, he enrolled at the University of Western Ontario. While in Ontario, he also worked with James Reaney, a playwright and poet. Tomson graduated with a bachelor's degree in music in 1975.

After graduating from the University of Western Ontario, Tomson began working as a social worker with Native groups all across Canada. For seven years he worked with children from broken families, Native elders, prison inmates, and others. This involvement with Indigenous people made Tomson aware of the many problems they faced.

In the 1980s Tomson began writing plays with Native themes. The Aboriginal people he met during his time as a social worker were his inspiration. His plays were performed mostly at urban Native community centers and on reservations. During this same period he worked with various Native theater companies as an actor, director, and musical director.

In 1986 Tomson was acknowledged nationally for his play *The Rez Sisters*. In the play, seven Native women of varying ages from the fictitious Wasaychigan Hill Indian Reserve in northern Ontario go to the world's largest bingo game in Toronto. The story describes how they plan to get to the bingo game and how they actually get there. Along the

Tomson Highway

way, the women experience both discord and acceptance, and they become like sisters by the end of the trip. The play is about heartbreak and hope, and all the women's stories are humorous and provide insight into the positive values taught in Indian mythology.

In 1989 Tomson wrote the play *Dry Lips Oughta Move to Kapuskasing*, which takes place on the same Indian reservation as *The Rez Sisters*. The main characters are seven Native men who are mentioned in but do not appear in *The Rez Sisters*. The men band together to protest an all-girl hockey team that they see as a threat to their manliness. The play has much less humor and is less optimistic than *The Rez Sisters* because it deals with the issues of alcoholism and violence.

Both plays won the Dora Mavor Moore Award and the Floyd S. Chalmers Award, which acknowledge outstanding theater production. *Dry Lips Oughta Move to Kapuskasing* was the first Canadian play to receive a full production and extended run at the legendary Royal Alexandra Theatre in Toronto. Both plays have continued to be produced throughout the world, including off-Broadway in New York City, in Edinburgh, Scotland, and in Tokyo, Japan, where they are performed in Japanese.

Tomson was the artistic director of Native Earth Performing Arts in Toronto from 1986 to 1992, when it was the only professional Native theater company in Toronto and the only organization of its type in Canada. Since then, Aboriginal plays have been produced regularly in Canada, especially in Toronto.

After his two successful plays, Tomson wrote an autobiographical novel, titled *Kiss of the Fur Queen,* about two brothers. It is based on Tomson's and René's experiences and is set in a Catholic residential school where the boys are abused. One of the boys in the story becomes a pianist, like Tomson, and the other a dancer, like René. René, who danced the role of Nanabush in *The Rez Sisters,* died of AIDS in 1990.

The book received very good reviews, and Tomson was commended for addressing the issue of sexual abuse in Indian residential schools. It was hard for Tomson to write the book because doing so brought back many bad memories. Tomson was bitter about being abused, and he was angry because he was forced to speak English during his time at the residential school. Because of this, he wrote the novel in Cree and then translated it into English. As it turned out, writing the book helped Tomson heal emotionally.

Tomson has also written three children's books, *Caribou Song, Dragonfly Kites,* and *Fox on the Ice.* All three are beautifully illustrated and written in Cree and English.

In 2004 Tomson was invited to give a presentation at a conference held by Soundstreams, a Canadian center for international music collaboration. His presentation was about the Cree language and his belief that all human language is a musical instrument. At the time, the creator of Soundstreams asked Tomson to write the words for a Cree opera. Four years later, in 2008, Tomson wrote *Pimooteewin* (The Journey), which is based on a classic First Nations myth. It's believed to be the first opera sung in Cree. With music by Montreal-based composer Melissa Hui, the opera was produced at Toronto's St. Lawrence Centre for the Arts.

Tomson has led a very busy life. Along with writing books, plays, and an opera, he has been writer in residence at the Universities of British Columbia, Montreal, and Toronto; Concordia University; Simon Fraser University; and many others. He has also taught Aboriginal mythology at the University of Toronto, where he holds the post of adjunct professor and teaches when he is on campus about one month every year. Tomson has conducted readings, lectures, and piano concerts all across Canada and in the United States and Europe. In total, he has traveled to more than fifty-five countries.

He enjoys combining readings and lectures with piano playing. Sometimes he plays solo, and other times he invites singer or musician friends and colleagues to join him. Most of the songs he plays are songs he has written, and the lyrics are in Cree. His songs have been translated into eleven languages.

Tomson spends his summers in a cottage near a lake in Ontario, and he winters at a seaside apartment in the south of France. When he reflects on his life, he realizes it did not turn out like he thought it would when he was a six-year-old boy helping his father in the outdoors, and he calls his life "a celebration of survival."

Selected Works of Tomson Highway

BOOKS

Comparing Mythologies. University of Ottawa Press, 2003.

Fox on the Ice. HarperCollins, 2003.

Dragonfly Kites. Harper Trophy Canada, 2002.

Caribou Song. Harper Trophy Canada, 2001.

Kiss of the Fur Queen. Doubleday Canada, 1998.

PLAYS

Ernestine Shuswap Gets Her Trout, 2004.

Rose, 2000.

The Incredible Adventures of Mary Jane Mosquito, 1991.

A Ridiculous Spectacle in One Act, 1990.

Annie and the Old One, 1989.

Dry Lips Oughta Move to Kapuskasing, 1989.

The Sage, the Dancer, and the Fool, 1989.

New Song, New Dance, 1988.

The Rez Sisters, 1986.

MONOLOGUE

Aria, 1987.

OPERA

Pimooteewin (The Journey), 2008.

AWARDS AND HONORS

National Aboriginal Achievement Award, 2001.

Maclean's magazine's one of the one hundred most important people in Canadian history, 2000.

Order of Canada, 1994.

Joseph Bruchac

When he was in the second grade, Joe Bruchac began writing poetry and giving it to his teacher, Mrs. Monthony. One day after she read one of his poems to the class, some of the bigger boys got jealous of the attention Joe was getting, so they beat him up after school. "That was my first experience with hostile literary critics," he jokes.

Despite this early experience, Joe kept writing poems all through grade school and high school, but never with any formal instruction or for a class assignment. He just did it because he loved it. And he didn't stop. For decades, he has written poetry, short stories, novels, and music that reflect his Native heritage.

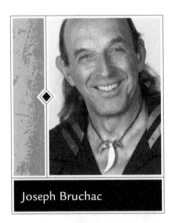

Joseph Bruchac

Joe grew up in Greenfield Center, New York, in the foothills of the Adirondack Mountains near Saratoga Springs. His grandfather on his mother's side, Jesse Bowman, was Abenaki Indian. Joe spent his early years living with his mother's parents, who played a key role in raising him. Eventually, Joe and his parents moved to a farm two miles away, but Joe continued to spend a lot of time with his grandparents. His grandmother, Marion Dunham Bowman, was a Methodist and a Mayflower descendant. Although she was a graduate of Albany Law School, she

MAYFLOWER DESCENDANTS

A Mayflower descendant is a person who can trace his or her heritage back to the 102 Pilgrims who sailed from England to America on the ship named the *Mayflower*. The Pilgrims established Plymouth Colony in Massachusetts in 1620. Nearly half of the colonists died during their first winter in America.

The General Society of Mayflower Descendants was founded in 1897. Only people who can trace their ancestry to a Mayflower passenger are approved by the Historian General and admitted into the society.

never practiced law. Her house was filled with books, and Joe loved to read.

Joe's grandfather knew how to read the forest. Joe followed him into the woods as soon as he was able to walk and learned as much from his grandfather's silences as he did from his words. Jesse taught Joe how to move quietly through the forest and look and listen for all the different creatures that lived there.

Everyone loved Jesse because he was a gentle man and a good listener. Although he could barely read and write, he ran the general store, where Joe loved to work and hang out. He rang up purchases and washed customers' cars. In the colder months, he sat and listened to the local farmers and lumberjacks tell stories around the wood stove. Joe's autobiography, *Bowman's Store: A Journey to Myself,* weaves together scenes from his childhood with his firsthand knowledge of American Indian cultures.

Joe's father was of Slovak ancestry. His family came from Slovakia, a small country in central Europe. He was a taxidermist, which is a person who prepares dead animals for display.

He was fascinated with Native people, and he took his children to tourist attractions run by Native American guides. Many of the guides became Joe's friends. His father also took Joe hunting and fishing.

When Joe entered high school, he was already a black belt in Indonesian martial arts, but he still considered himself a geek. He was a wrestler in junior high school and was on the wrestling team in high school. He also played football and participated in track events. He continued to wrestle in college and was a heavyweight wrestler on the varsity team. To this day Joe stays active in martial arts.

After he graduated from high school, Joe went to college at Cornell University in Ithaca, New York. It was around that time he began memorizing stories told by his Native elders. Joe knew that someday when he had children of his own, he would want to share the stories with them. It wasn't until after his children were born that he began writing the stories down.

In college, Joe's major for the first three years was wildlife conservation management. He always loved the natural world and still feels a deep connection to it. He would have preferred to major in writing, but he didn't see how he could make a living as a writer.

Up until the time Joe began taking creative writing courses and attending poetry workshops at Cornell, he had been a self-taught poet. Three weeks into one of his writing classes, his professor told him to give up writing because he would never write a good poem. Far from being discouraged, from that point on Joe ate, slept, and dreamed poetry. He eventually switched his major to English because he loved creative writing, and he even became editor of the school's literary newspaper. His early poetry was about nature, but he expanded into writing about American Indian themes. He wanted to portray his own Native people honestly, using stories he heard in his youth as a source of inspiration. He also tried to counter the bad images of Native people that other writers had created.

After completing his bachelor's degree from Cornell, Joe won a creative writing fellowship at Syracuse University, where he earned a master's degree in literature and creative writing. He continued his education and earned a PhD in comparative literature from Union Institute and University (formerly The Union Institute) in Ohio. For eight years, he taught creative writing and African literature at Skidmore College in Saratoga Springs, New York, not far from his hometown.

Joe also taught creative writing to the inmates of Great Meadow Correctional Facility, a maximum-security prison in Comstock, New York. Skidmore College hired him to create a writing program for the inmates, and Joe found it was quite easy to inspire the prisoners. He discovered that while the inmates lacked formal education, they had a deep hunger for personal growth. The inmates really wanted to make something of their lives, and they got tremendously excited about poetry and literature.

Joe realized the class meant more to the inmates than it did to most of his college students: "A college class in prison meant literally life and death to a prisoner in a way that it often doesn't to students in their late teens or early twenties who may not fully appreciate the opportunity that a college education offers them. I was always inspired by those men and women I worked with in prisons, and I remain inspired by them to this day."

Joe and his wife, Carol, cofounded the Greenfield Review Literary Center and Greenfield Review Press, where he has edited and published a number of highly praised anthologies of contemporary poetry and fiction. He finds inspiration as a writer by publishing the books of other authors. He feels the energy of other authors and believes this energy is part of his own personal journey as a writer and storyteller.

Joe has written 120 books for adults and children, and many of them have won awards. His books include picture books, poem collections, plays, short stories, and novels for children and young adults, and his work has appeared in more than five hundred publications, including *National Geographic* and *Smithsonian* magazines.

Much of Joe's work is written for younger readers. *When the Chenoo Howls: Native American Tales of Terror* is a collection of short stories that Joe wrote with his son James. The twelve tales are based on legends and mythical creatures described in the oral tradition of the Northeast Woodland Indians, a group of eight tribes. The tales are for children who love horror stories as well as tales about bravery, honesty, and clear thinking. In the stories, the heroes and heroines overpower monsters to achieve happy endings.

March Toward the Thunder is a novel for young readers based on the wartime experiences of Joe's great-grandfather. He says, "Interestingly enough, talking about a multicultural experience, my great-grandfather was a soldier in the American Civil War in the campaign of 1864 in Virginia. He was Abenaki Indian. He came from Canada, enlisted, and joined the Fighting 69th, the Irish Brigade. He was an American Indian in a group of soldiers who were largely Irish immigrants."

Joe continues, "When I was a child, we would make trips down to Virginia to visit relatives and walk across those battlefields without my really knowing much about it except the whole general history of the Civil War we were given in school at the time. But it made me want to know more and to do the research to find out the story in real depth. That particular story turned out to be one that was much more complicated and interesting than I had even thought it was when I started working on it."

Joe also has written a number of picture books for children, including *Sacajawea* and *Pushing Up the Sky*. An editor suggested he write Sacajawea's story, so Joe read all twelve volumes of the Lewis and Clark journals and more than one hundred books about Sacajawea. He traveled hundreds of miles of the route that Lewis and Clark took with Sacajawea as their guide, and he corresponded with tribal members of Sacajawea's nation, the Shoshone. He worked with Wayland

THE LEWIS AND CLARK EXPEDITION

The Lewis and Clark Expedition began in 1804 with the goal of finding an all-water route across America. President Thomas Jefferson appointed Meriwether Lewis and William Clark to lead the expedition. In November 1805, the explorers returned to Washington, DC, with all the information and specimens they gathered during their journey.

Large, Shoshone tribal historian, and consulted with Sacajawea's descendents.

Sacajawea, which was published in 2000, blends history with a personal look at the woman herself. Joe structured the book from two different storytelling perspectives, using both the voices of Sacajawea and William Clark. Writing the story this way created more depth than using only a single narrator or third-person narrator.

"We have two ears so we can hear two sides of every story," Joe says. "The chapters in the book are back and forth between William Clark's and Sacajawea's voices. Clark's voice is that of a man who is keeping a journal and writing. Sacajawea's voice is that of a woman who is a storyteller." In the book, Sacajawea tells stories to her child about her journey.

Joe wrote and published *Pushing Up the Sky* in 2000 when another editor asked him to write a book of plays for children based on Native American stories. The scripts are drawn from tales told by the Abenaki, Cherokee, Cheyenne, Ojibwe, Snohomish, Tlingit, and Zuni, and are accompanied by brief introductions to each tribe and its culture.

Having published more than one thousand poems over the last four decades, Joe says his favorite is always the poem that he's trying to complete. But he confesses to having a special fondness for *Thirteen Moons on Turtle's Back,* a picture book of poems that he and his good friend Jonathan London created together with artist Thomas Locker.

Joe has received many honors, including the National Endowment for the Arts Writing Fellowship and the Rockefeller Humanities Fellowship. He was also honored with the Cherokee Nation Prose Award and is the recipient of the Lifetime Achievement Award from the Native Writers' Circle of the Americas. In addition, he was awarded the Hope S. Dean Award for Notable Achievement in Children's Literature, the Knickerbocker Award, and the Wordcraft Circle Writer of the Year Award for *Bowman's Store.*

Continuing the Native American oral tradition, Joe performs in Europe and throughout the United States as a professional storyteller. He is featured at events such as the National Storytelling Festival in Jonesborough, Tennessee, and a comparable festival in England. He also performs storytelling programs at dozens of elementary and secondary schools every year and has been storyteller in residence for organizations and schools throughout North America. Joe's storytelling is simple and compelling. His traditional stories of life in the Abenaki culture pull listeners inside the tale and leave them wanting to hear more.

"I do feel that there is something that is found in traditional storytelling; the storytelling helps to strengthen the culture and the individual," Joe says. He thinks literature can do the same by awakening the imagination and helping readers see other points of view.

When he goes to storytelling events, Joe usually takes along a drum and flute and starts his performance with a song. He doesn't plan what he's going to do; instead, he lets the audience and the moment guide him. He has observed Native elders do the same when they tell stories, not preparing but trusting that the words will come to them in the right way.

When Joe speaks with groups of people, both young and old, he very often hears misconceptions about Native people.

"One of them," he says, "is that American Indian people are part of the past but not part of the present, and that the only way to be a real Indian is to appear in dress and behave as a Plains Indian would in the mid-1800s. I think that false impression does an injustice to people who are, like everyone else, buried in their experiences and in their background, and yet their heritage is of great importance to them."

Joe, who is now a grandfather himself, lives in the same house on the ninety-acre tract of land where he grew up with his grandparents. Working in an upstairs room, he's never at a loss for things to write about. "I'm inspired by many different things," Joe says. "Often, I'm inspired by experiences I've had, books I've read, people I've met, and stories I've heard." Sometimes Joe's ideas come to him in dreams, as with the 2001 book *Skeleton Man,* which is based on an Abenaki monster story.

Joe continues to read and listen to stories from the elders, and the central themes in his work are simple ones: that we should listen to and respect each other and the earth, and that we never know people until we know what is in their hearts. A disciplined worker, he typically writes a few hours each morning. When working on a novel, he tries to create at least three to five new pages a day in addition to editing previous pages.

In thinking about his creative writing process, Joe says, "In creating a fictional character, I hear and see that character. I feel as if that person is making their own decisions and I'm just taking notes. Often, I don't know what the characters will do until they've done it."

Joe and his two grown sons, James and Jesse, along with Joe's sister, Margaret, continue to work extensively on projects that preserve Abenaki culture, language, and traditional Native skills. All four are well-known and respected storytellers of traditional Native stories. Among them, they have published hundreds of publications, ranging from books for adults and children to academic essays.

Together they also perform traditional and contemporary Abenaki music as the Dawnland Singers. They began performing in 1993 and were featured at the Abenaki Cultural Heritage Days in Vermont. Their shows feature new and traditional northeastern Native music mixed with Abenaki storytelling.

All of the songs they write, whether in English or Abenaki, are meant to honor the elders, warriors, and past and present leaders. The music also honors Iraq War veterans and the great American Indian athlete, Jim Thorpe.

Joe has passed on his love for poetry to his son Jesse, with whom he recently spent time working on a series of poems. Their simple, sometimes narrative poems are written first in English and then translated into Abenaki, or vice versa. Joe writes in English, and Jesse, who has become quite good in the Abenaki language, writes the Abenaki translation.

Joe remembers a moment when Jesse was about seven years old. His son was walking through the upstairs hall of their house where Joe had covered one wall with poetry postcards. "I could just live for poetry," Jesse remarked. Many years later, Joe asked him if he remembered that day almost thirty years ago. "Of course," Jesse said. "I still feel that way. Poetry is the highest form of human expression."

As a poet, Joe believes in reading widely and writing regularly. He feels that expecting and accepting rejection is part of the deal, but says poets don't give up if they are serious about their work. He understands that almost all good writers (and most great ones) have been rejected at one time or another in their careers. Joe suggests that young people with aspirations to become writers find competent advisers who know what good poetry is. Sharing work with them and making thoughtful use of their constructive criticism can lead down a path of growth.

When giving advice to young people about how to succeed in life, Joe says, "I believe we have to look first to ourselves, to do our best. Then we can look to our families, our friends, and our close circle. We move outward in those circles ring by ring, like the rings made by a pebble dropped into the water. But if we look first at the vastness of the ocean around us, we may lose hope and see no purpose in our small strivings, our little lives. Yet everything is there in that first small circle, and the ripples made by the small pebble may touch some very distant shores."

When asked how he would like to be remembered, Joe replies, "If there is one way that I would want to be remembered, it would be as a voice for the people rather than as one who spoke only for himself."

Selected Works of Joseph Bruchac

FICTION

Night Wings. HarperCollins, 2009.

March Toward the Thunder. Penguin Group, 2008.

Code Talker: A Novel about the Navajo Marines of World War Two. Dial Books for Young Readers, 2005.

Skeleton Man. HarperCollins, 2001.

NONFICTION

Bowman's Store: A Journey to Myself. Penguin Group, 1997.

FOLK STORIES

When the Chenoo Howls: Native American Tales of Terror (with his son James). Walker & Company, 1999.

The Story of the Milky Way: A Cherokee Tale. Dial Books for Young Readers, 1995.

Turkey Brother and Other Tales: Iroquois Folk Stories. Crossing Press, 1975.

PICTURE BOOKS

Buffalo Song. Lee & Low Books, 2008.

Crazy Horse's Vision. Lee & Low Books, 2006.

Pushing Up the Sky. Dial Books for Young Readers, 2000.

Sacajawea. Harcourt, 2000.

Between Earth & Sky: Legends of Native American Sacred Places. Harcourt Brace & Company, 1996.

The Earth Under Sky Bear's Feet: Native American Poems of the Land. Philomel Books, 1995.

A Boy Called Slow: The True Story of Sitting Bull. Philomel Books, 1994.

The First Strawberries: A Cherokee Story. Dial Books for Young Readers, 1993.

POETRY AND ESSAYS

Lasting Echoes: An Oral History of Native American People. Silver Whistle, 1997.

Thirteen Moons on Turtle's Back. Penguin, 1992.

Good Message of Handsome Lake. Unicorn Press, 1979.

AWARDS AND HONORS

Native Writers' Circle of the Americas Lifetime Achievement Award, 1999.

Wordcraft Circle Writer and Storyteller of the Year, 1998.

Knickerbocker Award, 1995.

Hope S. Dean Award for Notable Achievement in Children's Literature, 1993.

Cherokee Nation Prose Award, 1986.

Rockefeller Humanities Fellowship, 1982.

National Endowment for the Arts Writing Fellowship for Poetry, 1974.

Maria Campbell

Maria Campbell is a best-selling author who is known worldwide. Her first book, *Halfbreed*, was published in 1973 and tells her life story. She left out nothing: the poverty, drug addiction, alcoholism, and physical abuse she endured throughout her young life are revealed. The term half-breed is offensive and refers to people of mixed heritage, especially the offspring of whites and Native Americans. Her half-breed status caused many problems for Maria in her early years. Much to her despair, she found that she was rejected by both First Nations and white people, both of whom disliked half-breeds.

Maria Campbell

Halfbreed is considered a literary classic and one of the greatest books ever written by a woman. The book has influenced generations of Native men and women, and today it is still one of the most popular books being used in high schools throughout Canada. *Halfbreed* has an important message for schoolchildren because it identifies half-breeds as people who live between two cultures; it reminds readers that the term half-breed is hurtful and should not be used thoughtlessly.

Maria's parents had a mixture of English, French, Irish, Scottish, and First Nations heritage. People with this kind of

THE MÉTIS

The Métis are a group of Aboriginal people in Canada who have both European and First Nations heritage. Métis people may have English, French, Irish, and Scottish heritage combined with Algonquin, Cree, Maliseet, Menominee, Mi'kmaq, Ojibwe, and Saulteaux heritage. Today, most Métis people have Métis parents rather than one parent with European heritage and one with First Nations heritage.

Métis people draw from both the Indian and European ways of life to meet their needs. Like other Aboriginal peoples, Métis suffer racism and prejudice. Because they are not entirely Indian or non-Indian, Métis struggle with their identity, and they sometimes present themselves as non-Natives to avoid racism.

Today, people who were, or are, rejected by both Native and non-Native cultures often find a home in the Métis community. Métis do not define themselves through bloodlines as First Nations people do. Rather, they are a community that celebrates two cultures.

mixed heritage are called Métis (see sidebar, above). Maria was born during a blizzard in April 1940 in a broken-down government shack, and she grew up in a road allowance community (see sidebar, page 63) near Park Valley, Saskatchewan.

When Maria was young, it was a common but inaccurate belief that all Métis men were alcoholics who beat their wives. Maria's father enjoyed drinking alcohol but was not abusive to his wife or his children. Her parents loved and respected one another. They both loved music, so the children learned to dance and play musical instruments, such as guitars and fiddles. The family went on long vacations to visit relatives, many of whom were full-blooded Indians. However, these relatives did not respect Maria's parents, and even though

Maria's family was invited fo Indian festivals, they never really fit in.

As a child, Maria enjoyed sitting in the kitchen listening to the old people tell stories. Her family was large and included grandfathers, grandmothers, aunts, uncles, and cousins. One day Maria walked into a room where her grandmother and some old women were telling stories. Speaking Métis, one of the old women asked Maria to tell a story. She did, and the old women told her that she was a wonderful storyteller. Maria savored the compliment and right then and there, she decided she was going to be a storyteller when she grew up.

Even though her family life was happy, Maria faced racism in her neighborhood. When German and Swedish immigrants first came to settle homesteads near where she lived, Maria thought they were rich and wonderful people. But she soon discovered that they looked down on the Métis and could behave cruelly. They regarded the Métis as a downtrodden and strange group of people who lived on creek water, gophers, and maple syrup.

Neighbors weren't the only people who mistreated Maria and made fun of her; her siblings also were cruel at times. As a little girl she liked to pretend she was Cleopatra, but her

ROAD ALLOWANCE PEOPLE

Road Allowance People were Métis who lost their land and were left with nowhere to live except the side of a road. The Canadian government owns the strips of land beside the roads in case the roads ever need to be widened. Métis families set up homes and communities on these narrow sections of land, which are typically only thirty feet deep. The last road allowance community in Winnipeg was disbanded in 1959.

brothers told her she was too dark skinned. They said that only her light-skinned cousin could portray Cleopatra. Because of her childhood experiences, Maria grew up thinking that white-skinned people were better than her. Other Métis had similar feelings: many light-skinned Métis moved into white neighborhoods and hid the fact that they were half-breeds in the hopes of making their lives easier.

When Maria was only twelve years old, her mother died. This was the beginning of the worst time of Maria's life. Because she was the oldest girl, she quit school to take care of her six brothers and sisters. Authorities constantly threatened to place all of the Campbell children in an orphanage. To prevent this, Maria married a white man when she was fifteen years old. Her plan to keep her family together didn't work, however, because her husband was an alcoholic who abused her and eventually reported her to the authorities. Her brothers and sisters were removed from Maria's home and placed in foster care.

After losing her siblings, Maria moved with her husband to Vancouver, British Columbia. Soon after, her husband abandoned her, never to return. This left Maria with no means of support and no money. She was a beautiful young woman, and because she was desperate for money, she became an expensive prostitute. Eventually, she began using drugs and alcohol. Her life kept going downhill, and she got involved with dangerous people who dealt drugs for a living. Maria became depressed; she tried to commit suicide twice, and she was hospitalized after having a nervous breakdown. Immediately after leaving the hospital, she joined Alcoholics Anonymous. With their help, and her determination, she quit drinking alcohol altogether.

Maria not only began to turn her life around, but she also began writing her book, *Halfbreed.* She thought that telling her story would help her recover from the alcohol and drugs, and she wanted people to know what it was like to grow up as a half-breed woman. There was nothing pretty about her story.

While she was writing, her life once again became difficult. She ran out of money, and with no work experience, she began to think about resuming work as a prostitute. She resisted, however, and instead began writing her book as a letter to herself, recording the story of the first thirty-three years of her life.

Many people who read *Halfbreed* say the book is very moving and often brought tears to their eyes or made them laugh. Maria is not bitter about the racism in her life, so she wrote the book in an effort to help people understand what racism and poverty feel like. The poverty Maria describes is different than the poverty experienced by millions of other people; it is the very specific type of poverty that comes from growing up as a half-breed, overwhelmed by feelings of desolation, shame, and hopelessness.

Maria writes about the white people in town who didn't want half-breeds in their church and recounts her own experiences to demonstrate how badly the white people treated her and the other Métis people. She describes unjust government policies that forced Métis to live in poverty and endure terrible living conditions in road allowance shacks. She writes about how Métis women were victimized, abused, disliked by other groups of women, disrespected by their husbands, and undereducated. Most of all, she tells her story, the story of a Métis woman who fights for equality in a man's world.

One time when Maria had no money, she decided to go to the welfare office for assistance. A friend who had been there advised her to act dumb, timid, and very thankful. She also told her to dress shabbily and even gave Maria an old coat that she called "a welfare coat."

Maria wore the ragged coat, old boots, and a scarf to the welfare office. She wanted to look like an old squaw to fit the stereotype of an Indian women. After she answered a lot of questions, Maria was given a voucher for groceries and bus tickets. The social worker told her to find a cheap apartment and not waste government money. When Maria walked out of the welfare office, she felt dirty and more humiliated and ashamed than she had ever felt in her life.

Later, when she lived by herself in Vancouver, Maria made friends with people of her own background and culture. As Maria met more educated people from other countries and other cultures, she began to gain confidence in herself. Many of her new friends were active in politics. Because of their influence Maria began bringing books home from the library. Although she was still feeling inferior, she gained confidence in her abilities as she read about the history of Native people.

As time went by, Maria used her feelings of anger, frustration, and shame as tools in her work as an educational and political activist. She founded the first women's halfway house and the first women's and children's shelter in Edmonton, Alberta. She has worked with Aboriginal organizations all across Canada and has set up food and housing co-ops. She has formed women's circles and worked with Aboriginal youths in community theater, and she has hired and supported Native people in the arts and theater. She is an advocate for Aboriginal justice and teaches Métis history and methods.

After the success of *Halfbreed* and her other books, including books for children, Maria tried another kind of writing and became a playwright. Her inaugural play, *Flight*, was the first all-Aboriginal theater production in Canada. Since *Flight*, she has also written, produced, and directed six other plays. Two of the plays toured all over Canada and were also performed in Denmark, Italy, and Scotland. For twelve years, from 1985 to 1997, Maria, along with her brother and daughter, operated a production company call Gabriel Productions. During that time, she produced and directed seven documentaries and the first weekly Aboriginal television series in Canada. The series was titled *My Partners, My People*.

Maria has been inducted into the Margaret Woodward Theatre Hall of Fame and has received a Distinguished Canadian Award by the Seniors University Group and the Seniors

Education Centre of the University of Regina. The award recognizes older adults who have made outstanding contributions to Canadian life. In 2004, Maria received the Thomas Henry Pentland Molson Prize of $50,000 from the Canada Council for the Arts. She was a unanimous choice for the award for her work as an author, storyteller, and playwright.

Maria, now a mother, grandmother, and great-grandmother, is retired from the University of Saskatchewan, where she taught Native studies. A popular guest speaker throughout Canada, the Unites States, and Australia, she speaks four languages. She prefers to think of herself as a community worker rather than a writer.

Selected Works of Maria Campbell

BOOKS

Stories of the Road Allowance People. Theytus Books, 1995.

The Book of Jessica. Coach House Press, 1989.

Achimoona. Fifth House, 1985.

Riel's People: How the Métis Lived. Irwin Publishing, 1978.

Little Badger and the Fire Spirit. McClelland and Stewart, 1977.

People of the Buffalo: How the Plains Indians Lived. J. J. Douglas, 1976.

Halfbreed. Saturday Review Press, 1973.

FILM AND VIDEO

Journey to Healing. Writer-director, 1995.

Joseph's Justice. Writer-director, 1994.

La Beau Sha Sho. Writer-director, 1994.

A Centre for Buffalo Narrows. Writer-director, 1987.

My Partners, My People. Coproducer, Canadian Broadcasting Company, 1987.

Cumberland House. Writer-director, 1986.

Road to Batoche. Writer-director, 1985.

Sharing and Education. Writer-director, 1985.

Red Dress. Writer, National Film Board, 1977.

Edmonton's Unwanted Women. Writer-director, 1969.

AWARDS AND HONORS

Officer of the Order of Canada, 2008.

Distinguished Canadian Award, 2006.

Saskatchewan Order of Merit, 2006.

Thomas Henry Pentland Molson Prize, 2004.

Margaret Woodward Theatre Hall of Fame, 2001.

National Aboriginal Achievement Award, 1995.

Golden Wheel Award, Rotary Club, Saskatchewan, 1994.

Saskatchewan Achievement Award, Government of Saskatchewan, 1994.

Gabriel Dumont Medal of Merit, 1992.

Floyd S. Chalmers Award for Best New Play, 1986.

Dora Mavor Moore Award, 1986.

Order of the Sash, Métis Nation of Saskatchewan, 1985.

National Hero, Native Council of Canada, 1979.

Vanier Award, Vanier Institute, 1979.

Honorary Chief, Black Lake First Nations, 1978.

Nicola Campbell

Nicola Campbell has a strong respect for First Nations culture, languages, spirituality, and tradition, and she draws on all of these when she writes adult and children's short fiction and poetry. She explains, "I heard an elder speak of the importance of our languages and our culture. He said that our words are powerful, our stories are elastic, our languages are music; they dance, they move, and they are medicine for our people. He said they are a spirit within themselves, and we are only the channel that brings them to life. I write because I know what he said is true."

Nicola was born on November 5, 1972, in Edmonton, Alberta, and raised in the Nicola Valley as a member of the Nicola Valley Indian Band in Merritt, British Columbia. Her father was Cree and Métis and grew up in Saskatchewan. Her mother's family is Interior Thompson Salish.

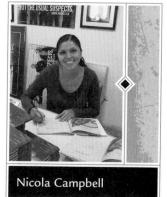

Nicola Campbell

Life was not easy for Nicola's family. Her father died when she was a young girl, and her brother died in 1999 when he was only fourteen years old. Fortunately, Nicola had her mother and a large extended family for support and guidance. Her family would have gatherings and tell stories, many of which were about her aunts' and uncles' experiences at Indian residential schools. These stories eventually inspired her writing.

When she was growing up, Nicola hunted, fished, and gathered food. She liked to be outside, climbing around in the bushes and getting dirty in the creeks. She enjoyed nature, and being outdoors was a big part of her life.

Nicola also enjoyed visiting her grandfather's farm, where his pigs chased her and her siblings around the farmyard. Her grandfather had a huge garden she used to invade to eat strawberries, raspberries, and peas. Her mother also had a garden, and Nicola routinely raided that as well. She got home from school before her mom got home from work, so she would go into the garden and eat all the peas. It would not be long before her secret was discovered. When her mother got home from work, she would go into the garden to get something for dinner, but instead she would find all the pea husks Nicola left behind.

Through hard work and determination, Nicola's mother became an inspiration for her daughter. When Nicola was growing up, her mother struggled to make ends meet, but she was determined to care for her children and make her way in the world. She eventually became a teacher and went on to become a school principal.

Reading is one of Nicola's favorite activities, and she describes herself as a "bit of a bookworm." When she was young she was always reading a book. She read books inside her desk at school and in her bed with a flashlight. She even tried to read in the car but always ended up getting carsick.

In addition to reading, Nicola liked to write, but she was afraid to share her stories. She thought they were stupid. Still, she wrote in her journal every day. She wrote poetry, stories, memories, and even random thoughts.

"I wrote about what I saw in the sky and on the land," she says. "I wrote what people said and the teachings our elders told us. I wrote about random sounds, smells, thoughts, angry, happy, sad, hurt, excited, whatever. I wrote everything."

Nicola had many favorite authors when she was a child: "It is hard for me to pick one favorite, but some of my favorite authors include Judy Blume, David Eddings, and Maria Campbell. And seeing as I'm still growing up, some of my recent favorites are Christopher Paolini and J. K. Rowling."

One of the authors that Nicola mentions is her aunt, noted author Maria Campbell (see chapter 8, page 61). "She was a big inspiration to me," says Nicola. "I decided I wanted to be an author when I was about seven years old, but school was not easy for me. I struggled through school and found out that you don't have to be a brainiac to do what it is you really want to do. You just have to be determined and you will find a way."

Books written by her aunt and other Native authors inspire Nicola. She loves reading books about Native people and people of color. She also loves to hear stories about culture, spirit, and medicine. The stories and words passed on to her by her ancestors and elders become part of her. In turn, she shares them in her stories so her readers can learn from them.

She explains, "That's who we are, that's what we descend from as Indigenous people. We are not static, we are not solid, we are fluid and so were our ancestors. We've learned to live in these other ways, but we can still transform, just as our words do."

Nicola attended North Kamloops High School in British Columbia. She had a tough time in school. She could certainly speak English, but English as a school subject involving grammar and literature was very difficult for her. She failed English in both high school and college. She also had other problems during her teen years, including drinking and going to parties all the time. Both got out of hand.

It is easy to understand how Nicola became involved in drinking and the party scene. When she was young, many members of her extended family were alcoholics. Growing up in a large, desolate area in central Canada, she was exposed to alcohol, drugs, and violence all around her. But Nicola knew she had to get her life straightened out so she could pursue her dreams, and she did. She stopped drinking when she was seventeen. At the time she was one of the only people in her life who didn't drink. Now many members of her family have stopped drinking and using drugs, and they are forging a trail of healing for their children to follow.

After high school, Nicola attended the University of British Columbia. Although her grammar wasn't very good, she made it through her first years of college. During her freshman year, she was asked to do class assignments called freewriting. A timer was set for ten minutes, and the students were told to write randomly and nonstop, recording whatever they thought of, including memories, stories, or poetry. They were instructed to keep writing and not lift their pens from their pages, and they were not allowed to fix grammatical errors or reread what they wrote. It was during these exercises that Nicola found her voice as a writer.

Her first published book, *Shi-shi-etko,* began as a writing assignment for her Writing for Children class in the creative writing program at the University of British Columbia. She initially didn't have a specific storyline in mind; she just sat down to write. She put the story away for a year and would occasionally revisit and edit it. She admits to being a very slow writer, and it's normal for her to work on a poem or story for a few years.

The following year, one of her classmates asked Nicola about her story *and* if she had named her main character yet. She hadn't. It was very important to her that the character have a First Nations name, so one night she prayed about it. That night she dreamed of the name "Shi-shi-etko." She woke up, wrote it down, and phoned her aunt Delia to ask if the word could possibly be a name. Her aunt said yes, it could be a name, and it would mean something like "she plays in the water" or "she loves to play in the water."

Nicola asked many elders in her community if they had ever heard the name before. She was told there was one family whose grandmother had a similar name, but it was unclear if it was the exact same name. When she spoke with the family, she asked for permission to use the name and was told that because of the way the name came to her, it was okay. So she named the main character Shi-shi-etko, which is a phonetic spelling that Nicola chose to allow for easier pronunciation.

Following much encouragement from her family, friends, and classmates, Nicola finally sent her story to a publisher for consideration. Her brother had recently died, and she was at a crossroads in her life. She had already failed almost an entire year of the Native Indian Teachers Education Program at the University of British Columbia, but she decided to apply to the university's creative writing program and was accepted. Nicola knew she eventually wanted to go into teaching, but her first goal was to write. Her family questioned her dream of being a writer; they were concerned that "writers starve." When *Shi-shi-etko* was accepted for publication as a children's picture book, Nicola knew she would continue as a writer.

The book is about a young girl who has to leave her family and the life she knows to attend residential school. Shi-shi-etko spends her last days at home listening to her mother, father, and grandmother share valuable teachings they want her to remember. She listens carefully so she can remember what she's been taught, then she and other children are put into the back of a pickup truck and taken to the school.

"My goal with the story, *Shi-shi-etko,* is that it awakens people, and opens eyes and hearts to the impact of residential schools on our Aboriginal children and families," Nicola explains. "My hope is that children of all nations everywhere can understand that no matter who they are, no matter where they come from, they are sacred. I want them to be inspired by this sacredness and to always be proud of who they are and where they come from."

Nicola's second children's picture book is the sequel to *Shi-shi-etko* and is called *Shin-chi's Canoe*. Shi-shi-etko is about to return to the residential school for her second year, leaving behind her parents and grandmother, who are upset about the separation. But this time she is not alone. Her six-year-old brother, Shin-chi, is going too. As they begin their journey in the back of the truck, Shi-shi-etko tells her brother about all the things he must remember. He won't see his family again until the salmon return in the summertime. Shin-chi clings to a miniature toy canoe, keeping it close until one day at school he decides to let it go to float down the river.

Nicola Campbell

"Writing *Shin-chi's Canoe* was definitely a challenge," Nicola says. "I knew when *Shi-shi-etko* was published the story wasn't finished, and I had to tell the rest of the story. When I wrote *Shin-chi's Canoe*, it was with the awareness that I wanted to honor my elders, family, and survivors for the immense strength of spirit it took them to 'survive' residential school, for what it took to persevere despite all the sorrows, trials, and tribulations they were faced with. To carry forward the love for our languages, cultures, and traditions, and pass our values, beliefs, and way of life on to our future generations. If it were not for their steadfast determination and love of all that is 'us,' we would have nothing."

Nicola graduated with a bachelor of fine arts in creative writing. She is currently working on a master of fine arts degree and writing her thesis about biographical poetry. In her free time, Nicola writes adult and children's short fiction, poetry, and screenplays.

RESIDENTIAL SCHOOLS

The residential, or boarding, school system in Canada was founded in the 1800s. By 1884 education became compulsory for Aboriginal children under the age of sixteen. If parents refused to send their children to school, they risked facing time in prison.

The United States opened residential schools for Indian children about the same time as Canada. The first schools in the United States were started by Christian missionaries. The Bureau of Indian Affairs was established in 1824 and opened additional schools.

Both in the United States and Canada, the schools forced the assimilation of Indian children into white society. Indian students' hair was cut, they were not allowed to speak their Native language, and they could not practice religious ceremonies. Many students suffered physical and emotional abuse at the hands of their teachers.

The Canadian government closed the last First Nations residential school in 1996. All the large Indian residential schools in the United States have also been closed, although a few small schools remain open.

Nicola lives a drug- and alcohol-free lifestyle. She also is active and likes the outdoors, just as she did as a child. She loves biking and hiking, and she has participated in traditional cedar dugout war canoe racing for sixteen years. She currently lives in North Vancouver with her preschool-age son.

"My goal in writing," says Nicola, "is to remind children that no matter who they are, no matter what happens in their life, no matter where they go, they should always be proud of who they are, never be ashamed of their identity, and know that they are loved."

Selected Works of Nicola Campbell

CHILDREN'S BOOKS

Shin-chi's Canoe. Groundwood Books, 2008.

Shi-shi-etko. Groundwood Books, 2005.

POETRY

"I Would Have Gone to War." *Yellow Medicine Review*, 2008.

"Buckle Up Shoes." *Sky Woman: Indigenous Women Who Have Shaped, Moved, or Inspired Us*. Theytus Books, 2005.

"Lullabies." *Sky Woman: Indigenous Women Who Have Shaped, Moved, or Inspired Us*. Theytus Books, 2005.

"Nle7kepmxcin." *BC Studies*, 2001.

ESSAYS

"Where Have My Huckleberries Gone?" *Ubyssey Newspaper*, 2003.

AWARDS AND HONORS

Marilyn Baillie Picture Book Award Finalist, 2009.

TD Canadian Children's Literature Award, 2009.

Ruth Schwartz Children's Book Award Finalist, 2006.

TD Canadian Children's Literature Award, 2006.

Anskohk Aboriginal Children's Book of the Year Award, 2006.

Marilyn Baillie Picture Book Award, 2006.

Tim Tingle

Book reviewers call Tim Tingle "a true tale spinner" and "a superb storyteller." Tim was born on November 24, 1948, in Houston, Texas, to Margaret, a Chickasaw, and Archie Tingle Jr., a Choctaw. Tim has three brothers and one sister. He's an enrolled member of the Choctaw Nation of Oklahoma. Prior to the Trail of Tears, the Choctaw Nation was one of five major tribes of the southeastern United States. The other four were the Cherokees, Chickasaws, Muskogee (Creek) Nation, and Seminoles.

Tim's grandmother, Mawmaw, was very important to Tim when he was a child. She was married to an Irishman, and their house was a gathering place for the whole family. In 1915 when she was a young mother, Mawmaw was struck and blinded by a rock thrown by a boy who didn't like Indians.

When Mawmaw was a child, she was sent to a boarding school where she was punished for speaking the only language

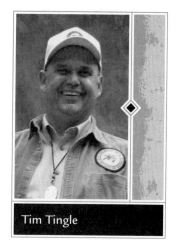

Tim Tingle

she knew, Choctaw. That lesson stayed with her throughout her life. Since she was bullied because she was an Indian, she believed it was dangerous to acknowledge being a Native American. That's why she never taught her grandchildren the Choctaw language. In fact, although Tim knew he was Choctaw, it wasn't talked about much in his home.

Tim spent weekends at his grandparents' house and had an ordinary childhood. He and his siblings gathered eggs, played on the swing set, and had mock sword fights. Tim remembers rows and rows of corn planted in the field near the house.

His father and uncles didn't want Tim to grow up without being taught the old ways, so they took him on trips to Big Thicket, a heavily wooded area in southeast Texas. This was before it became a national preserve in 1974, with over 105,684 acres of public lands. Tim remembers seeing bears, wolves, and snakes in the woods. He and the men would hike for a day and then make camp. Carrying canteens, coffee, sugar, and eggs, they fished and hunted for food. They ate off tin plates and cleaned them with leaves.

These trips would last for several days, and Tim and his male relatives got completely away from town and family influences. No women were allowed. Tim learned the Choctaw customs while sitting around the campfire in the evenings listening to Choctaw stories. His father and uncle spoke Choctaw, and Tim picked up a word or two. At home he learned Choctaw songs by listening to his grandmother sing them. But it wasn't until he was a student at the University of Oklahoma that he finally learned the Choctaw language.

Tim has always been a writer. He wrote his first play in the second grade. The class was having quiet time and he was supposed to be coloring, but instead he was writing a screenplay about his favorite television show, *Zorro*. The teacher caught him and asked if she could read it to the class. When he agreed, she read it aloud and made fun of him. "I never forgot that experience," he says. "I walked away thinking it was never all right to write stories down."

Even though he promised himself he would never again write down a story, he realized he could still *tell* a good story: "I have always been a talker of tales and made up the most unbelievable lies as a child to get out of trouble. I soon discovered that if the lie was completely outrageous, my mother would laugh and shake her head, call her best friend on the phone to tell her 'my crazy story,' and often forget to punish me."

"When I began writing in the second grade, I first wrote short plays which my friends and I would act out in our backyard playground," Tim continues. "By high school I wrote poetry but was too afraid to show it to anyone. I think this early fascination with poetry gave me a vital appreciation for the importance of every single word on the page."

After graduating from South Houston High School in Pasadena, Texas, in 1966, Tim went to the University of Texas at Austin. He graduated in 1974 with a bachelor's degree in English. He later went to the University of Oklahoma, where he earned his master's degree in Native American studies in 2003. After that, he was awarded a graduate teaching fellowship at the University of Oklahoma.

During his studies at the university, Tim learned Choctaw writing. He had access to many resources and databases with information about the Choctaw. As a result of his research, he had historical evidence on which to base his Choctaw stories. His knowledge of the Choctaw culture gives his stories more impact and power.

Tim accidentally discovered how much he loves storytelling. When he realized his son was not being taught Choctaw history in elementary school, he volunteered to tell his Choctaw stories to the kids in his son's class. He told the students stories based on his family's memories, which not only entertained them but also taught them important history they would not have learned otherwise. Tim found a new calling.

To improve his speaking skills, Tim joined a Toastmasters club in Austin, Texas. Toastmasters is an organization that helps its members improve their communication, public speaking, and leadership skills. When it was Tim's turn to speak at meetings, he shared his Choctaw stories. He soon realized it was his vocation to assemble Choctaw history and legends and put them into stories to be passed through the generations.

Tim's stories are inspired by childhood and life experiences along with interviews he conducted with Choctaws in Texas, Oklahoma, Mississippi, and Alabama in the early 1990s. Tim recorded over one hundred stories. He would write the stories down and then listen to the recordings again, revising the stories if necessary.

He also wrote stories down before performing them. He knew he'd be able to remember them better if he wrote them down first. "I felt 'writing to perform' was different than just writing stories down," he says.

Over time, Tim came to realize that he needed to write down his Choctaw stories so they could be saved and shared. He doesn't want the stories to stay exclusively in the inner circles of a family or pass away with the one who knew them best. He wants stories to be retold among many people of all cultures. He believes the Choctaw stories are important because they are not only about hardship but also about triumph and the determination of the human spirit.

When comparing written stories to oral storytelling, Tim doesn't favor one above the other. He has always thought of himself as a storyteller, even though his first career was writing. He writes his own performance stories and updated versions of Choctaw folktales, so his writing skills are important. Even though the stories he tells are written down, Tim never tells them exactly the same way. Tim believes that in a live performance, there is a closeness that exists between the storyteller and the audience that can never be duplicated by writing a story on paper. However, he does admit that a book will outlive the spoken word and can be read and appreciated long after the author is gone.

Once when Tim attended a reenactment of the Trail of Tears (see sidebar, page 83), he met an older man named Charley Jones, the official storyteller for the Choctaw Nation

Tim Tingle telling stories

and a Choctaw Council member. At the reenactment, many people walked thirty miles in honor of the hardships their elders endured during their rough journey. Tim walked fifteen miles with Charley and listened to the many stories he told him. Some of the stories later became books.

Charley was familiar with the art of storytelling, and he tutored Tim in this skill. One important lesson he taught Tim was not to be discouraged when he is telling a story and there are empty seats in the audience. Charley told Tim that he's not only speaking to the people who are present but also to those whom the stories are about. "Sometimes, in my mind, I actually imagine who from my family might be there," Tim says.

Through his guidance, Charley strengthened Tim's skills significantly. "He was the most important mentor of my life," says Tim.

Tim retraced the route of the Trail of Tears to the Choctaw homelands in Mississippi and began recording stories of the tribal elders. This resulted in his first book, *Walking the Choc-*

TRAIL OF TEARS

The Trail of Tears was the forced relocation of many Native American tribes from the southeastern area of the United States to the Oklahoma Territory. The purpose of the relocation was to open up twenty-five million acres of land for white settlements. During the journey, thousands of people, especially children and the elderly, died from exposure to the elements.

The Choctaw were moved in three groups. When the first group finally arrived in Arkansas, an *Arkansas Gazette* reporter interviewed a Choctaw chief who was quoted as saying the Choctaw removal had been "a trail of tears and death."

taw Road. In 2005 the book was awarded Book of the Year in both Oklahoma and Alaska, marking the first time in history that one book had been selected by two states in the same year. Tim completed a tour of eighty Oklahoma libraries that year, presenting stories from his book and promoting literacy throughout the state.

Walking the Choctaw Road is a collection of eleven short stories and includes a special Trail of Tears memory as told by his great-great-grandfather, John Carnes, who survived the trail in 1835. The book is currently studied in universities across America and in other countries.

Fellow writer and friend Joseph Bruchac (see chapter 7, page 50) says *"Walking the Choctaw Road* is like an old Choctaw chant that will stay with you and lend you some of its strength. Cross the river with these stories, and they will give you safe passage."

Tim also is the author of *Spirits Dark and Light: Supernatural Stories of the Five Civilized Nations.* Released in October of 2006, the book includes ghost stories from the Cherokee,

Chickasaw, Choctaw, Creek, and Seminole nations. One of the stories, "The Lady Who Changed," won a 2007 Storytelling World Resource Award.

Tim has coauthored three books with fellow storyteller and author Doc Moore. *Spooky Texas Tales, Texas Ghost Stories: Fifty Favorites for the Telling*, and *More Spooky Texas Tales* were published by Texas Tech University Press. *More Spooky Texas Tales* is set in modern times and includes scary stories for fourth- through seventh-grade readers.

When Turtle Grew Feathers is Tim's first early childhood read-aloud book. It's an American Indian version of *The Tortoise and the Hare*. The story is a favorite for young children through second graders, and Tim often performs it at the National Storytelling Festival in Jonesborough, Tennessee. The book features colorful illustrations by California artist Stacey Schuett.

Crossing Bok Chitto was released in 2006. The title refers to a river that cuts through Mississippi. In the days before the Civil War, the river was a boundary. The Choctaws lived on one side, and the plantation owners and their slaves lived on the other. If a slave escaped and made his way across the river, the slave owner couldn't follow, and the slave was free; that was the law.

The book is about Martha Tom, a young Choctaw girl. Although she knows better than to cross the river, one day when she is out picking blackberries she disobeys her mother and finds herself on the other side. She meets a young slave boy named Lil Mo and his family. When Martha discovers the mother is to be sold, she helps Lil Mo and his family escape across the river to freedom.

Crossing Bok Chitto was Tim's first illustrated book; it won many state and national awards and was the inspiration for two award-winning plays. It was picked as a 2006 Editor's Choice by the *New York Times Book Review*. Illustrated by Cherokee artist Jeanne Rorex Bridges, it won the 2006 Oklahoma Book Award for both author and illustrator, becoming the first book in the history of the award to win both categories. It was also given the 2008 American Indian Youth Literature Award.

Tim wrote a biography that he called *Saltypie,* which is a word Tim's father invented to mean any sort of pain or distress. Published as a picture book, it is a family tale of Indian struggles and triumphs in the twentieth century. Tim flawlessly weaves the connecting threads as he talks about the amazing endurance his family had throughout the generations.

His closeness with his grandmother, Mawmaw, is evident in the family photos that are included in the book. Choctaw artist Karen Clarkson did the illustrations and wonderfully portrayed Mawmaw at different stages in her life. In the book, Tim recalls being six years old and realizing his grandmother was blind and that her blindness was the result of a racially motivated attack. He also recalls a hospital vigil years afterward when she received an eye transplant.

Saltypie was published in 2010 by Cinco Puntos Press and was selected as an American Library Association Notable Book for 2011. It was also chosen as a 2011 Notable Book for a Global Society by the International Reading Association.

When it comes to writing stories for children, Tim says, "Children are fascinated without being analytical, and a child's mind is a sweet sea of imaginative thinking. I like to see the lights come on when a child is reading or listening to a story. They also enjoy the excitement of a good ghost story and are not too proud to show their fear. They shiver and wrap their arms around themselves; they laugh nervously and then flood the author with cool and thoughtful questions at the climax of the tale."

Tim recently contributed to a new book, *Trickster: Native American Tales: A Graphic Collection,* which was recommended as a 2011 Young Adult Library Services Association Great Graphic Novel for Teens. His story "Rabbit's Choctaw Tail Tale" is included in the book. "It's the most widely known and often-told Choctaw story," says Tim. "It's the favorite story of my mentor, Charley. I've been performing this story for over twenty years, though this is the first time I've written it as a story. There are hundreds of trickster rabbit stories, but this simple tale provides an easy-to-understand social lesson."

Tim believes the trickster is an important character in any story. "Tricksters are everywhere, they aren't just in American Indian tales, and they are alive and well today," says Tim. "Tricksters are celebrated in American Indian culture; they are labeled as 'troublemakers' in Western culture. The trickster steps back to observe social norms; they see the humor in social situations. They know it's healthy to laugh at serious situations. They're willing to suffer the consequences of being a trickster. Trickster stories are critical because they let us observe through the eyes of humor. There's value in humor; it shouldn't be squashed. This can be insightful for young adults who are labeled troublemakers in school. Never hurt others with your humor, but never underestimate the joy of a life filled with laughter."

Tim performs and is a guest instructor at the National Museum of the American Indian at the Smithsonian. He is also a regular speaker at the American Library Association's conferences, and he performed at their 2008 multiethnic concert, "Many Voices, One Nation." In addition to completing several speaking tours for the US Department of Defense, Tim has performed for children and military personnel in Germany.

Tim is a strong advocate for literacy. He delivered a keynote address before the board of the National Education Association in Washington, DC, in 2010, presenting a new approach to American Indian history curriculum. Tim's work has been recognized by former president George H. W. Bush and included in his Presidential Libraries Education Program.

Tim keeps busy storytelling, writing folklore, and teaching Native American cultural workshops at universities, schools, and conferences. Every Labor Day for the past several years, he has performed a traditional Choctaw story before Chief Gregory Pyle's Annual State of the Nation Address at the tribal gathering in Tushkahoma, Oklahoma. This Choctaw event attracts over ninety thousand people. In 2004 Tim founded the Choctaw Storytelling Festival, a three-day event that is held annually in Oklahoma and draws Choctaws of all ages for several days of sharing memories and traditions. He also performs Choctaw stories and related tribal music, both contemporary and traditional, at festivals throughout the country. He carries the book *The Mercy Seat* by Rilla Askew in his drum bag. He loves the story, and it's one of his favorite books.

When he is not performing, Tim likes to relax and write on the shores of Canyon Lake, Texas, where his house overlooks the canyon and lake. He also likes to read or spend a day at the San Antonio Zoo with his grandson.

Tim believes you should make your writing matter. "My editor and I once argued for four days over a single comma in a story, a single comma which was holding up the publication of the book," he says. "We laugh about it now and are proud that writing matters so much to both of us."

He gives this advice to aspiring young writers: "Learn to listen. Keep your eyes and ears open to everything around you. Listen to how people talk. Learn how to become part of the scene and step out of the scene and observe. Write what you know. But don't limit your experience to what you know now."

Selected Works of Tim Tingle

BOOKS

Saltypie: A Choctaw Journey from Darkness into Light. Cinco Puntos Press, 2010.

Crossing Bok Chitto: A Choctaw Tale of Friendship & Freedom. Cinco Puntos Press, 2006.

Spooky Texas Tales. Texas Tech University Press, 2005.

Texas Ghost Stories: Fifty Favorites for the Telling. Texas Tech University Press, 2004.

Walking the Choctaw Road: Stories from Red People Memory.
Cinco Puntos Press, 2003.

The Collector. Authorhouse, 2003.

Song of the Night. Authorhouse, 2002.

The Choctaw Way. Storytribe Publishing, 1997.

AUDIO RECORDINGS

Live & Thriving at the 30th National Storytelling Festival.
National Storytelling Press, 2003.

AWARDS AND HONORS

American Library Association Notable Book, 2011.

Notable Book for a Global Society, 2011.

American Indian Youth Literature Award, 2008.

American Library Association Notable Children's Book, 2007.

Storytelling World Resource Award, 2007.

New York Times Book Review Editor's Choice, 2006.

Oklahoma Book Award, 2006.

Alaska Reads Book of the Year, 2005.

Oklahoma Reads Oklahoma Book of the Year, 2005.

Writers' League of Texas Teddy Award, 2005.

International Storytelling Center Teller in Residence, 2004.

If a URL takes you to a general resource, do a search on the site to find specific information about the author.

For information on how to get your work published:

Your Name in Print: A Teen's Guide to Publishing for Fun, Profit and Academic Success. Elizabeth Harper and Timothy Harper, St. Martin's Griffin; 2005.

For more information about Native American writers, visit:
infoplease.com/spot/aihmbioaz.html
library.illinois.edu/edx/nativeamericanchildrens.htm
native-languages.org/literature.htm
wordcraftcircle.org

For more information about First Nations writers, visit:
digital.library.upenn.edu/women
library.ubc.ca

For more information about Sherman Alexie, visit:
fallsapart.com
goodreads.com
pbs.org/moyers/journal
topics.nytimes.com
yalsa.ala.org

For more information about Louise Erdrich, visit:
answers.com
gale.cengage.com
notablebiographies.com
pbs.org/moyers/journal

For more information about Joseph Boyden, visit:

bookbuffet.com

cbc.ca

josephboyden.com

penguingroup.com

quillandquire.com

straight.com

For more information about N. Scott Momaday, visit:

achievement.org

bookrags.com

cliffsnotes.com

enotes.com

imdb.com

okhumanities.org

For more information about Marilyn Dumont, visit:

12or20questions.blogspot.com

athabascau.ca

banffcentre.ca

thewriterscollective.org

For more information about Tomson Highway, visit:

athabascau.ca

banffcentre.ca

cbc.ca

enotes.com

quillandquire.com

tomsonhighway.com

For more information about Joseph Bruchac, visit:

childrensliteraturenetwork.org

ipl.org

josephbruchac.com

loc.gov/podcasts

For more information about Maria Campbell, visit:

athabascau.ca

enotes.com

esask.uregina.ca

firstnationsdrum.com

For more information about Nicola Campbell, visit:

cbc.ca

groundwoodbooks.com

lookingforwardlookingback.com

similkameenspotlight.com

For more information about Tim Tingle, visit:

artofstorytellingshow.com

timtingle.com

ttupress.org

yalsa.ala.org

Front Cover:

Tim Tingle: Courtesy of Tim Tingle

Joseph Boyden: Courtesy of Yves Tennivin

Louise Erdrich: Courtesy of Bettina Strauss

Marilyn Dumont: Courtesy of Brandon University

N. Scott Momaday: Courtesy of OMA&D Ethnic Cultural Center

Sherman Alexie: Courtesy of David Bedard

Tomson Highway: Courtesy of Tomson Highway

Page 1: Courtesy of Seattle Municipal Achieves

Page 6: Courtesy of Changing Hands Bookstore

Page 9: Courtesy of Minnesota Historical Society

Page 17: Courtesy of Shelly Lietheiser

Page 20: Courtesy of Yves Tennevin

Page 24: Courtesy of Toni Tucker

Page 27: Courtesy of OMA&D Ethnic Cultural Center

Page 32: Courtesy of OMA&D Ethnic Cultural Center

Page 35: Courtesy of Marilyn Dumont

Page 38: Courtesy of Marilyn Dumont

Page 43: Courtesy of Tomson Highway

Page 46: Courtesy of Tomson Highway

Page 50: Courtesy of Joseph Bruchac

Page 61: Courtesy of Celebration of Women

Page 69: Courtesy of Groundwood Books

Page 74: Courtesy of Nicola Campbell

Page 77: Courtesy of Tim Tingle

Page 81: Courtesy of Tim Tingle

Kim Sigafus is an award-winning freelance writer and photographer from Warren, Illinois. She is an Ojibwa and her family is from the White Earth Indian Reservation in the northwest region of Minnesota.

Her journalism background includes work for newspapers in Illinois, Iowa, and Wisconsin. She also writes romance, fiction, short stories, poetry, and children's books. Her nonfiction work includes *The Life and Times of the Ojibwa People*, released in 2011, which she cowrote with Lyle Ernst. She was published in the 2010 edition of *Writer's Digest's Photographer's Market*.

Kim Sigafus

Her awards include the Media Specialist Award and the Lena D. Myers Award for her work at the *North Iowa Times*, and the Faith and Freedom Award in the photography and poetry category for her poem "Not Today." She's currently working on a script for a musical.

Lyle Ernst is a member of the Native American Coalition of the Quad Cities based in Moline, Illinois. He is a freelance journalist and has contributed news stories, feature stories, and columns to various newspapers, including the *Cedar Rapids Gazette, Clayton County Register, Waukon Standard*, and *Allamakee Journal* in Iowa, and the *Prairie du Chien Courier Press* in Wisconsin. Currently, he is freelancing for the *Moline Dispatch, Rock Island Argus*, and the *Review* in Illinois. Lyle has had articles published in *Radish, Our Iowa*, and *Women's Edition* magazines. He has contributed essays to four books edited by Robert Wolf: *An American Mosaic, Jump Start: How to Write from Everyday Life, Heartland Portrait*, and *River Days: Stories from the Mississippi.*

Lyle Ernst

In addition to editing fiction and nonfiction, Lyle has co-written a novel and is working on the biography of a Wisconsin rock-and-roll band. He resides in Davenport, Iowa, with his wife, Pat, and TT, a rambunctious miniature dachshund.

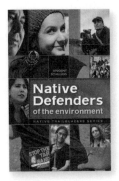

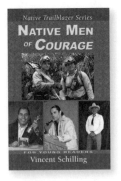